Also available at all good book stores

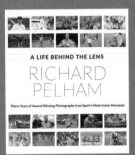

A LIFE BEHIND THE LENS
RICHARD PELHAM
Thirty Years of Award Winning Photography from Sport's Most Iconic Moments

9781785315466

The Beautiful Badge
THE STORIES BEHIND THE
FOOTBALL CLUB BADGE

MARTYN ROUTLEDGE
& ELSPETH WILLS

SPORTS BOOK
AWARDS 2019
WINNER

9781785313929

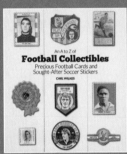

An A to Z of
Football Collectibles
Precious Football Cards and
Sought-After Soccer Stickers
CARL WILKES

9781785315602

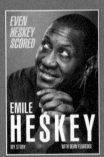

EVEN
HESKEY
SCORED

EMILE
HESKEY
MY STORY   WITH DEAN ELDREDGE

9781785315008

MASTERING

LEE
SCOTT

9781785315633

STEVEN SCRAGG

A TOURNAMENT
FROZEN
IN TIME
European Cup Winners' Cup

9781785315381

FOOTBALL'S
50
MOST IMPORTANT MOMENTS

FOOTBALL'S
50
MOST IMPORTANT MOMENTS

- From the writers of the Football History Boys blog -
BEN JONES
& GARETH THOMAS
@TFHBs

First published by Pitch Publishing, 2020

Pitch Publishing
A2 Yeoman Gate
Yeoman Way
Worthing
Sussex
BN13 3QZ
www.pitchpublishing.co.uk
info@pitchpublishing.co.uk

A CIP catalogue record is available for this book
from the British Library.

ISBN 978 1 78531 632 6

Typesetting and origination by Pitch Publishing
Printed and bound in India by Replika Press Pvt. Ltd.

Contents

Introduction

Football is more than just a game. Over the last 150 years it has become a source of identity, conflict and debate for all those who follow and play it. It has reached the farthest corners of the globe and boasts more players and supporters than any other sport. In this book, we will be going right the way through the illustrious, colourful and often tragic history of football and finding out what the most important moments are in this truly beautiful game.

We will start with the game's origins. By looking at public schools, the football association and the question of rules, we can then move comprehensively through the decades. Much of what makes football the game we know and love today stems from the early decisions made in the Victorian era as professionalism took over and competitive tournaments were introduced. By the turn of the century, the beginnings of football's global appeal became apparent. With the British Empire continually expanding, football followed with it to each and every corner of the world.

Football would come to represent more than just the 11 men on the pitch. It would capture the hearts and minds of communities across the world, becoming a source of identity to the millions who watched. By 1900, the game's great amateur sides were gone and football was well and truly the 'people's game'. The players, often from working-class backgrounds, became idolised by fans both young and old. Their time in the limelight would lead to calls for unions and players' rights. This would continue throughout the century.

By the start of the First World War, football had become a common ground amongst nations so opposed in ideologies. It would even become a symbol of hope on the battlefields of France and Belgium. Throughout the war, the Football League in England was suspended, leading to the women's game being introduced to large crowds across the nation. Initially to raise morale for the war effort, the skill and guile of those playing led to the sport reaching staggering heights of popularity. By the end of the war, the Football League had returned and an FA ban was placed on women playing at FA grounds. It would be decades before this changed.

Technological advances, sped up by war, brought transportation and mass media into new realms. Planes, faster ships and more easily available automobiles meant the world was getting smaller. Domestically, the mass production of the radio meant supporters could listen to the beautiful game from the comfort of their own homes. By 1930 football's unwavering popularity meant FIFA would have its first World Cup and the question of which nation was the greatest on Earth was answered. Outside of football, a similar question was being asked by different nations with increasingly extreme ideologies. The Second World War would once again call upon footballers to play their part.

Following the war, commercialism and new money led to attendances continuing to rise before the mass production of the television meant the game could be watched in households across the world. The late 1950s and 1960s would bring social revolution and a cultural change to a new generation of players and supporters. Football continued to grow with the European Cup and championships leading to high-quality matches and tactical styles never seen before. Football was to have its first superstars and celebrities. In the UK, George Best epitomised how football and celebrity was closer than ever. Elsewhere, Ferenc Puskás, Pele and Alfredo Di Stefano ruled the game before new flair was seen in the progressive styles of Johan Cruyff's Ajax and Franz Beckenbauer's Bayern. Consecutive European Cups led to these teams being regarded as two of the best ever, and tactical changes saw some of the game's greatest managers.

But tragedy was never far away. In 1949 the impressive Torino team were taken from us too soon in the Superga Air Disaster, before Matt Busby's Manchester United side suffered a similar fate in Munich in 1958. By the 1980s, the Bradford Fire, Heysel Stadium Disaster and Hillsborough tragedy brought into question the standard of modern football stadia and people's attitudes towards football supporters. On the pitch, Diego Maradona introduced genius and controversy and British teams dominated the European Cup with Liverpool, Aston Villa and Nottingham Forest all winning 'Old Big Ears'. The 1990s saw football reach new levels. Television was now the leading source of news and communication for people around the world and large companies like Sky began to take their pick of the action. The Premier League split away from the Football League after 104 years and money was pumped into the sport on a scale unimaginable to those Victorian pioneers who codified the game.

As the standard of football improved alongside the stadiums in which it was played, football would expand its global franchise. By 2010 the poorest continent on Earth, Africa, would also play host to the World Cup, showing how a sport can bring everyone together in one language. The modern era of football would be defined by two players – Lionel Messi and Cristiano Ronaldo, both winning multiple Ballon d'Ors and Champions Leagues. Of course, there are a number of moments not even mentioned here, but we will see how certain moments have led to the changes we can see since 1857. Football is a sport which is ever growing and ever reflecting the world in which it is played. It is something we need to celebrate and better understand.

The purpose of this book is not to provide a definitive list. Its primary aim is to help to better understand the world of football all around us. Through the study and analysis of certain moments throughout football's history, we can better comprehend why the modern game is how it is. The list of 50 moments will no doubt be different for each and every individual who reads through and each opinion brings with it new weight, new arguments and new findings which will help to further the discussion around football history. If history has taught us nothing else, football is truly a game of opinions!

1857–85

1. Sheffield FC (1857)

2. The Formation of the Football Association (1863)

3. The First FA Cup (1871/72)

4. The First International – England v Scotland (1872)

5. The 'Disease' of Professionalism (1883)

1

Sheffield FC (1857)

There seems to be no better place to start than with the creation of football's oldest club – Sheffield FC. In 1857 football had seen a surge in popularity as public schools aimed to develop young men into physically fit and morally sound individuals. Seeing football as a perfect means to do so, amateur clubs began to appear across the country. Often comprised of public school alumni, Sheffield FC was no different. Amongst those to found the club were 'old boys' from the Sheffield Collegiate School. Originally introduced to the game by their college masters, these students included Nathaniel Creswick and William Prest, the co-founders and innovators of the 'Sheffield rules'.

Football had become a game played usually in the winter months. Called by some 'the winter game', it gave sportsmen a chance to put down their cricket bats and play a different sport more suited to all weathers. Indeed, in 1857 cricket was universally recognised as not just the national game, but the game of empire. Football was used first in Sheffield for these precise reasons, as a winter game for the local cricket club. It was the resulting Sheffield rules which would help create Britain's first footballing city. Described as a 'football boom', there is little to doubt the city's influence on the modern game.[1]

---

1   John Lowerson, *Sport and the English Middle Classes: 1870-1914*, (Manchester: Manchester University, 1993) p.82

In comparison to the version set up by the Football Association in 1863, the Sheffield rules defined *this* form of football. The list of 11 laws are at times similar and at others far removed from the game we watch today. In fact, when reading the rules it is almost reminiscent of rugby. The involvement of catching and passing the ball with the hands highlight where the initial problems in the game lay. However, the inclusion of only scoring via the foot and the removal of 'hacking' lends itself to a sport more at home with the Football Association's later vision.

The side itself was made up of 'young technologists, businessmen and future captains of industry'[2]. Such players are far removed from the modern-day interpretation of footballers and their respective backgrounds. Despite this, the inclusion of 'businessmen' introduces the idea of a middle-class player in contrast to the gentrified game of the southern public schools. With Sheffield being the only proper club in 1857, games would usually be between rival XIs from within the institution. This could be 'married vs singles' or 'professionals vs the rest'.[3] Following the close of their first season, *Bell's Life* reports that the Sheffield side hosted an athletic games at Bramall Lane.[4] Football clubs were already proving to be more than just the players that represented it. The event would become an annual tradition in Sheffield and help the game to grow. For football to thrive it would need to embrace the community around it and encompass the wider society in which it was played. Soon there would be 15 clubs in the Sheffield area all playing under Creswick and Prest's rules. Sheffield had become Britain's football capital.

So what of the earliest fixtures? The beginnings of the 'rules derby' dominate most narratives as local club Hallam faced their rivals for the first time in 1860. Although fixtures had been played before between club members, the founding

2   In Derek Birley, *Sport and the Making of Britain*, (Manchester: Manchester University, 1993) p.258

3   'History – Sheffield F.C.', *Sheffield FC*, https://sheffieldfc.com/history/

4   *Bell's Life and Sporting Chronicle*, 11 April 1858

of Hallam FC and the resulting matches between the two has seen it dubbed 'the oldest fixture in football'. Still contested to this day, the first match was played at Sandygate Lane on 26 December 1860. Sheffield emerged as 2-0 winners. Two years later, the sides met at Bramall Lane in a brutal encounter which saw the game descend into violence more than once:

'At one time it appeared likely that the match would be turned into a general fight, Major Creswick (Sheffield) had got the ball away, and was struggling against great odds—Mr Shaw and Mr Waterfall (Hallam). Major Creswick was held by Waterfall, and in the struggle Waterfall was accidentally hit by the Major. All parties are agreed that the hit was accidental. Waterfall, however, ran at the Major in the most irritable manner, and struck at him several times. He also threw off his waistcoat and began to "show fight" in earnest.'[5]

Although played for the love of their game, what this shows is that football was already an incredibly passionate pastime. It meant more than a kickaround. Indeed, it was about local pride, about bragging rights, and the presence of 'noisily jubilant' fans seems to confirm this.

The influence of Sheffield FC in the creation of the modern game cannot be understated. Indeed, Sheffield managed to create a genuine football culture in the wider local area and show how football could provide an identity to more than just the players on the pitch. Sheffield would become one of the most important institutions throughout the resulting 'sporting revolution'. Football's modern existence owes a great deal to the early pioneers in the 'Steel City'. There is no way that in 1857, when Nathaniel Creswick and William Prest founded the club, they could ever imagine just how influential it would become. Furthermore, they wouldn't have been able to predict the importance the founding of Sheffield FC would have on the 49 moments still to come. What they had achieved was the first chapter in one of modern history's greatest stories.

---

5   *Sheffield Independent*, 30 December 1862

2

The Formation of the
Football Association (1863)

By 1863 football (in its various forms) had become the sport of
public schoolboys and university students around the country.
Despite Sheffield's popularity, a consensus on rules was still
yet to be reached by the growing number of institutions who
played the game. With an increasing desire, particularly
amongst London-based sides, to play matches further afield,
the difference in rules across the country caused confusion
and needless disruption. It was not uncommon for teams to
play matches that switched rules and codes halfway through.

The most influential institution with regards to rules, and
particularly to the codified game which followed, was found
in Cambridge. Indeed, the earliest histories of football credit
Cambridge with the inspiration for the Football Association.[6]
The university had seen a number of rules published in the
first half of the 19th century, before a more uniform and
easily applied set was written in 1848 and again in 1856.
The prime motivation for such laws was the confusion which
spread throughout the university when students from different
schools, with different football rules, came together. What sets
Cambridge's rules apart from others at the time is the distinct

---

6   N.L. Jackson, *Association Football* (London, 1900) p.26

lack of handling. 'In no other case may the ball be touched with the hands.'[7]

To combat further uncertainty with the laws of the game, 12 clubs and schools met at the Freemasons' Tavern, London, on 26 October 1863. The aim was to discuss and agree upon a shared set of rules. Those involved were Barnes, Blackheath, Perceval House, Kensington School, Civil Service, Crystal Palace, Surbiton, The Crusaders, Blackheath Proprietary School, No Names of Kilburn, Forest and Charterhouse. It would be Ebenezer Morley of Barnes who proposed the formation of an association and the motion was carried by 11 votes to one. Charterhouse, although present at the meeting, declined to join the association.[8]

Following the acceptance of the codes of the game, the first match played under these rules took place in December that year between Barnes and Richmond. Despite being a 0-0 draw, the match drew particular praise for the simplicity of the rules and the excellence of each side in playing under them.[9] Although a successful first trial, the game was still yet to be truly agreed upon as certain laws caused debate for the next few years. Most rules were ratified, but the inclusion or exclusion of 'hacking' posed the greatest threat to the FA's infancy.

'Hacking' was the practice of kicking an opponent's shins in order to trip them up and regain possession. For some clubs, most notably Blackheath, its removal was a threat to the game's 'masculine toughness'. On the other hand, Morley was vocal in his support for the removal of the 'barbaric practice', citing that if it were to be included, players would be reluctant to play the game after leaving school.[10]

---

7   *Cambridge Football Rules*, 1856

8   Matthew Taylor, *The Association Game* (London: Routledge, 2008)

9   *The Field*, 26 December 1983

10   Richard Holt, *Sport and the British* (Oxford: Oxford University, 1989)

The removal of hacking would lead to another rival code of 'football' forming – rugby. In the modern day, we often think of the two sports as completely different rather than two codes of the same game, as they initially were. It is here where we begin to see the first use of the term 'soccer' to help supporters of both codes distinguish which sport they were to discuss and debate.

The FA's early growth was modest, with the rival code in Sheffield holding greater influence over the sport.[11] In 1867 the FA only had ten affiliated members and its very future was under threat. Rules still posed a problem almost five years into the association. *Sporting Life* regularly covered meetings and their contents. Frequently the issue of rules and possible changes took centre stage as members tried 'with much energy and labour to establish a code which shall meet the views of all'.[12]

There is an air of negativity around the FA and articles are often seen to 'wish' them success. There was no certainty as to the association's future, but the energy and effort exerted were seen by some as ample proof that rewards were just around the corner. By 1871 the Rugby Football Union had been established and gained immediate popularity, with over 20 clubs joining initially. The association game would need something big to swing the sporting tide their way. The next decade would be pivotal to the shaping of the modern game.

Football's origins at the Freemasons' Tavern are difficult to ignore. It is clear that without this moment the game we watch today could have been totally different. The success, if not immediate, of the Football Association in creating a governing body around a codified sport would lead to other games being developed and innovated over the coming decades. The social and cultural change centred on sport is what historians now describe as a 'sporting revolution'.

---

11 Matthew Taylor, *The Association Game*, p. 31
12 *Sporting Life*, 23 January 1867

3

The First FA Cup (1871/72)

The FA Cup is huge. Modern-day football fans are becoming increasingly unaware of its importance as more and more tournaments are introduced to us through TV and social media. In 1871 football was still very much in its infancy – an amateur sport played by gentlemen and public school alumni. Commonly referred to as the oldest club competition in football, the tournament's construction owes much of its development to two factors: firstly, the promotion of rugby and the RFU into a more popular institution and, secondly, the success of the Youdan Cup in Sheffield.

The first Youdan Cup Final in 1867 saw football reach new heights. Although played under Sheffield rules, the match between Hallam and Norfolk saw a record 3,000 spectators, each paying 3d, cram into Bramall Lane Cricket Ground.[13] These numbers offered unwavering proof of football's huge popularity.[14] It also becomes apparent that despite the FA being four years old by the beginning of the Youdan Cup, the large numbers of spectators in Sheffield demonstrates that the association game needed something to improve its own reputation.

---

13 *Sheffield Telegraph*, 6 March 1867
14 Adrian Harvey, *Football: The First Hundred Years* (London: Routledge, 2005)

Following the success of the Youdan Cup, secretary of the FA Charles Alcock launched his own competition. With no official league, a cup was the only way in which it could be decided who the best team in the association game was. Starting in November 1871, the tournament's early response was modest. Most reports were limited to scorelines with very little detail found within. Nevertheless, by the turn of the year, attitudes began to change as the competition reached its final stages. The final itself was previewed extensively by a number of leading newspapers, calling it a 'great event in the football world.'[15]

The first edition of the competition was won by The Wanderers at the Kennington Oval in south London. Meeting them in the final was the Royal Engineers, a team comprised wholly of military personnel. Winning 1-0 in front of a reported 2,000 spectators, the match was 'perfectly one-sided', due in part to the excellence of the Wanderers' side.[16] Attendance may have been bigger, but for the one shilling admittance. A year later, the Wanderers would retain the trophy at Lillie Bridge before the Royal Engineers eventually emerged victorious in 1875.

Despite its modern success, some commentators are quick to argue that we should not overestimate the initial success of the FA Cup – indeed, only 15 clubs entered the inaugural competition.[17] *The Morning Post*, although writing with a genuine excitement for the final, deemed the upcoming match as 'unsatisfactory'. With the Football Association not representing half of the football clubs in the country, it wouldn't provide a definitive answer to who was the strongest in the country.

Competition did help the game to grow, however. By 1872 the FA had in fact become 'large, extensive and powerful'.[18]

---

15   *The Morning Post*, 16 March 1872

16   *The Morning Post*, 18 March 1872

17   Matthew Taylor, *The Association Game* (London: Routledge, 2008)

18   *The Morning Post*, 16 March 1872

Sport was no more about playing for the love of the game. The will to win would soon outweigh antiquated beliefs of morality and honour around football. Clubs would spring up across the nation, particularly in the Midlands and further north. The lack of violence from within football, alongside the progressive Elementary Schools Act in 1870, meant the sport was to eventually be played in new schools across Britain. A new generation of footballers were about to take centre stage in football's incredible history.[19]

It would take ten years for the FA Cup to truly represent the whole nation, but once it did it would continue to grow to this day. Now, we see over 700 entrants each season from the Premier League to the lowest levels of the football pyramid. Through the FA Cup, football had begun to become the national sport, overtaking rugby's initial popularity. Without it, it is hard to see the subsequent development of the Football League and the general spread of the beautiful game to all corners of the globe.

---

19   Derek Birley, *Sport and the Making of Britain*, pp. 267-8

4

The First International –
England v Scotland (1872)

England has many international rivalries, but the one it shares with Scotland is perhaps stronger than any other. Going back centuries, the two nations have been at war, shared monarchs and disagreed on key issues – even today. By 1872, however, the rivalry could take to a new battlefield – a football pitch. The earlier introduction of the FA Cup had brought with it a new level of excitement and a competitive element to the game. With this would come spectatorship and inevitable growth.

England taking on Scotland was nothing new. In football's great rival, rugby, matches had indeed taken place between the two nations. In March 1871 a fixture was arranged at Raeburn Place in Edinburgh. The match was played under rugby rules, and although 20-a-side, it drew a reported 4,000 spectators to the ground. The popularity of rugby was unquestionable and with its own Rugby Football Union flourishing, there seemed little chance of the association game taking its place as the nation's new favourite. Scotland won the tie by a surprising 1-0 scoreline. The point-scoring system in rugby was yet to be fully functional.

If Edinburgh was the great city of rugby in Scotland, then Glasgow was its opposite. The first FA Cup had even seen a Glaswegian club play in the earlier rounds – Queen's Park. It is with Queen's Park where the basis of the first international lies. As Scotland's leading side, they agreed with the FA to take on a selection of England's finest players in Glasgow. Other Scottish players had been invited to take part but very few took up the offer.[20] Indeed, just a week before the match, *The Field* newspaper reported that the 'Scotch eleven' would be represented by players from various clubs across Scotland, like Glasgow Academicals and Dumfries.[21]

So what was the first international match like? The match was widely reported and recorded an attendance of between 3,000 and 4,000 spectators. Each report would also make specific notes about how the game was played by both sides.[22] Interestingly, one of the first notes found in the *Greenock Telegraph* is that England produced a 'heavier team'. It continues to note, however, that in the association game, this has little effect compared to the rugby code. Much of the article is devoted to explaining the rules of soccer with the Scottish public seemingly not as familiar with them as first thought.[23]

One key aspect of the early game, particularly with the English side, was dribbling. The ball being given to one player who would rush forward alongside the rest of his team – more reminiscent of a rugby scrum. The final score was 0-0, surprising when taken in comparison to other scorelines at the time. Scotland did strike the ball against the 'tape', however. Reports suggest that the incident split the crowd with many thinking a goal had been scored. With no crossbars in 1872, the calls for new technology were about to begin! No goals in 1872, but fortunately it was a result which was

---

20 Stuart Spencer, 'Scotland v England: The World's First Football International Fixture', *Scottish Football Museum* (30 November 2017) https://scottishfootballmuseum.org.uk/scotland-v-england-the-worlds-first-football-international-fixture/

21 *The Field*, 23 November 1872

22 *Sheffield Daily Telegraph*, 1872

23 *Greenock Telegraph and Clyde Shipping Gazette*, 3 December 1872

to only twice happen again. Overall, the game was a great success with Scotland drawing particular praise for holding their own against a 'picked' side of English players. What was anticipated for the next fixture between the two was a Scottish side with players from across the nation.[24]

Scotland would dominate the early results between the two nations, winning nine of the first 13 matches and scoring a staggering 43 goals. In comparison, England registered just two victories, with the more notable being a 5-4 win at the Oval in 1879. The progressive style of the Scottish side would attract fans from across Britain.[25] This in turn was to help football to become a true spectator sport. In comparison with the friendly atmosphere at rugby matches, the support for the association game was truly fanatical.[26] The match would become a regular feature in the British football calendar, with the Kennington Oval, Hamilton Crescent and eventually the first Hampden Park playing host to a multitude of fixtures. Attendance trebled by 1882 as 12,000 fans saw Scotland win 5-1 in Glasgow.

What this match had proved was that football was growing to be an international game and soon more and more nations would take it to their hearts. The game had introduced notions of national identity being tied up within sport. The teams of Scotland and England represented more than just the 11 on the pitch. This is indeed a theme which will recur throughout this book. In 1876 and 1882 respectively, Wales and Ireland quickly followed the example set by their neighbours and set up their own national teams. With the British Empire rapidly expanding, soon the association game would be played across the globe. Football became a leading player in the Victorian sporting revolution and, at last, its most popular.

---

24 *Greenock Telegraph and Clyde Shipping Gazette*

25 *Sheffield Telegraph*, 7 April 1879 – The piece notes the attendance of spectators from Sheffield, Birmingham, Wales and Manchester

26 Richard Holt, *Sport and the British* (Oxford: Oxford University, 1989) p.255

5

The 'Disease' of Professionalism (1883)

The FA Cup had spread its reach across the nation and football was growing considerably each year; the number of entrants had risen considerably from 15 in 1871 to 84 in 1883. Teams from England, Wales, Scotland and Ireland had entered the first round to prove football to be the 'national' sport. From Lancashire, Blackburn Olympic had entered the competition that season, playing the 'combination' game. This was a style of play, originating in Scotland, that focussed on using passing and build-up play compared to the more common 'kick-and-rush' tactics. What was perhaps more surprising at the time was the fact this team was made up of working-class players.

Football, as we have seen, was generally regarded as a game for gentlemen. But a mere 20 years after the establishment of the FA, it had managed to win the hearts and minds of working men, particularly in the north of England. Blackburn Olympic's 2-1 victory at the Kennington Oval against holders and amateurs Old Etonians was a victory for class as much as it was for football. The *Derby Daily Telegraph* was quick to draw upon the side's industrial roots in its write-up of the final. Quoting the Blackburn fans' 'strange' accents, it notes a chant of 'Coom, Olympics, put on another shovelful'. Perplexed, it passes this off as some 'manufacturing metaphor'.[27] The Northerners had won the cup, but soon after the victory questions would be raised.

Professionalism. In the modern day it seems as though football has always been a professional game, but in 1883 it was the source of fierce debate among teams and players across the nation. Upon its codification, the FA had never envisioned a professional game. They had thought the sport would only be played for pleasure and never for cash.[28] For many, professionalism was a threat to morality and the commercialisation of the game would mean winning was now more important than taking part. Arguably, the introduction of the FA Cup in 1871 had already started a move towards competition over leisure, but emerging stories about broken time payments to players brought the debate into households across the country.

Indeed, professionalism, at the time, was banned and clubs caught paying players would receive expulsion from the FA, like Accrington did in 1883. Broken-time payments were seen as part of a 'veiled professionalism'. Although not openly portrayed as 'professional', footballers were, in increasing numbers, receiving payments to cover the loss of their working wages in order to play the game. For the *Edinburgh Evening News*, this introduced questions as to the sportsmanlike nature of football and further evidence that 'certain clubs' would do whatever they could to, above all else, win.[29]

There was a genuine fear for the amateur game as professionalism grew and even leading figures from the game's creation like Charles Alcock admitted to the practice becoming inevitable.[30] Amongst those in opposition to proposals for the legalisation of professionalism was Sheffield FC. Describing

---

27   *Derby Daily Telegraph*, 2 April 1883

28   Richard Holt, *Sport and the British*, 1989, p.106

29   *Edinburgh Evening News*, 10 December 1884

30   Mike Huggins, *The Victorians and Sport*, (London: Hambledon, 2004) pp.64-5

the idea as inexpedient and unnecessary, they believed that every effort should be used to prevent it taking place.[31]

Ultimately, a meeting of the FA at the Freemasons' Tavern decided to allow professionals to play the game. The meeting involved proposals from the various local football associations, all with their own ideas as to how professionalism could be allowed. For some, the FA Cup's amateur status was one of the most important ideas, whereas others focussed their efforts on restricting the dissemination of the practice via geographical restrictions on where clubs could pick their players.[32]

Reservations towards the inclusion of paid professionals were numerous, but what they overshadowed was how this helped football to ultimately grow into the national sport. Despite its public school heritage, football's less violent nature had meant the working masses were more eager to play the game than rugby.[33] Alongside an ever-expanding middle class, the opportunity for profit and the eagerness to win meant the nature of the game had changed. Furthermore, since 1830 social legislation saw a rise in literacy rates, and by the 1880s it would become increasingly common to see arguments made by all in society. Professionalism was no doubt an idea with its roots embedded deep within class and social divides and newspaper articles can be found in support of it.

In a letter to the *Manchester Courier* in 1884, a Mr WC Warburton wrote of his support for professionalism within the game. He writes that the professionals (particularly from Blackburn) have helped to 'raise the standard of play'. He continues to note that Manchester people will be 'only too glad to pay for a true exhibition of the game'.[34] Warburton's letter is clear. For the general public, the inclusion of professional

---

31 *The Sportsman*, 8 December 1884

32 *The Sportsman*, 19 January 1885

33 Derek Birley, *Sport and the Making of Britain*, p.270

34 *Manchester Courier*, 3 November 1884

players had helped to improve the standard and thus see an increase in gate receipts.

Professionalism has left a long and chequered legacy on football and sport in general. Football, like most sports, had grown out of a love for recreation and playing for the sake of playing. In fact, in modern British soccer only one club remains with amateur status – Queen's Park in Scotland. Their club motto echoes this statement – *Ludere Causa Ludendi* (Play for the sake of playing). But with the sheer growth and popularity football enjoyed in its infancy, there is no shock in its later openness to commercial and financial ventures. With modern-day arguments around the purity of the game, it is important to realise that this is nothing new and that nothing is ever perfect. What football has offered, however, is a sense of purpose, belonging and solidarity, even in the face of economic might and influence. Will it continue to do so?

1888–1914

6

The Football League and Preston North End – The First 'Invincibles' (1888/89)

The Football League, the wonderful Football League, is over 130 years old. However, when founded in 1888, it was a bright new idea that was enabled by the acceptance of professionalism in the sport. Suddenly the game that had stolen the hearts of the working class was now a viable job choice and so a formal league was born.

After an initial meeting of the prospective new members in Anderton's Hotel, London, the Football League was officially agreed upon on Tuesday, 17 April 1888 in the Royal Hotel, Manchester. A 12-team league was set up with sides from the Midlands and the north of England, comprising: Preston North End, Blackburn Rovers, Bolton Wanderers, Accrington, Everton, Wolverhampton Wanderers, Derby County, Burnley, Aston Villa, West Bromwich Albion, Notts County and Stoke. Representatives, meanwhile, attended the meeting from Notts Forest, Sheffield Wednesday, and Halliwell, with Aston Villa's Scottish director William McGregor elected chairman.[35] At a later meeting of the Football League, it was decided that the title would be decided by a points system, where two points

---

35   *Blackburn Standard*, 21 April 1888

would be awarded for a win, one for a draw and of course nothing for a loss.[36]

The league would run from September 1888 till February 1889, with each side playing each other home and away. So, on Saturday, 8 September 1888, the first-ever round of the Football League kicked off. Preston North End hosted Burnley in front of 5,000 supporters. Preston comprehensively beat the visitors 5-2[37] before travelling to Wolverhampton Wanderers the following week to again win comfortably, 4-0. Preston topped the league, a position they would not relent all season.

In the following weeks Preston continued to sweep their opposition aside, beating Stoke 7-0 at home, courtesy of four goals from inside-forward Jimmy Ross. By the time they dropped their first point in October, they had gone six matches unbeaten. Accrington held North End to a 0-0 draw, but their momentum was not halted. By the end of the season Preston had won 18 of their 22 games, drawing just four times. They racked up 40 points, some 11 clear of second-placed Aston Villa. Centre-forward John Goodall (12 goals in 14 caps for England) was the top goalscorer with 21 goals in 21 games, becoming the first 'Golden Boot'. The Football League was here to stay and we won't forget the first invincible side in the first-ever campaign.

Preston were not just dominant in the league in 1888/89, the FA Cup was theirs too. The FA Cup (Moment 3) carried immense prestige for football clubs, the honour no doubt superior to the fledgling Football League title. The previous year Preston had destroyed Hyde 26-0 in the first round of the cup, finishing eventual runners-up to West Bromwich Albion. In 1888/89 they wanted revenge, and, if their league form was anything to go by, the desire for a first FA Cup win was a fair expectation.

---

36   *Sheffield Daily Telegraph*, 23 November 1888

37   *Sheffield Independent*, 10 September 1888

A 3-0 victory over Bootle in the first round was followed by a 2-0 win against Grimsby Town away from home. Birmingham St George's were dispatched in March 1889, before a semi-final rematch with last season's winners West Brom beckoned at Bramall Lane, Sheffield. A single strike separated the sides, Preston returning to the final for a second consecutive year, and they would face Wolverhampton Wanderers, who were also seeking a first FA Cup. Ross, Sammy Thomson and captain Fred Dewhurst all scored to write their names into the record books on 30 March 1889 at the Kennington Oval – the double was Preston's.[38]

This moment has earned its place due to the significance of Preston as England's first-ever invincible side. Until the end of the 2018/19 campaign, just Arsenal in 2003/04 have matched the league unbeaten status of Preston North End. Add to that the two times Celtic have achieved the feat in Scotland, along with the single season achievement of Glasgow rivals Rangers too and you have a very exclusive honour in British football indeed!

---

38   Bryon Butler, *The Illustrated History of the FA Cup* (London: Headline Book Publishing, 1996) pp.53-5

7

Scotland v England –
Ibrox Disaster (1902)

Sadly, our next moment is one of British football's first tragedies, the Ibrox Stadium disaster of 1902. The turn of the century had seen no relent in the love of the game across Britain, with crowds on the increase. International football became a big part of the sport, with the British Home Championship an absolute spectacle – Scotland, England, Wales and Ireland fighting it out every year since 1883/84, the rivalry and competitiveness fierce.

The Home Championships had proven to be highly successful. Attendances at games regularly began to reach levels above 25,000 spectators in the 1890s, especially in England and Scotland. At the turn of the century, Celtic Park saw 63,000 boisterous supporters see Scotland demolish the English 4-1. Even in rugby-loving Wales, figures began to reach above 6,000 in 1899 and 11,000 four years later. Such popularity meant matches were sometimes played at the home of Welsh rugby, the Arms Park.[39] These improvements to the game meant Wales began to register credible results against the might of England and Scotland.

---

39 *Manchester Courier and Lancashire General Advertiser,* 27 March 1900

Within Scotland itself, the Glasgow rivalry was still as strong as it is today. With the current Hampden Park (the modern national stadium) not built, Ibrox (Rangers) and Celtic Park (Celtic) battled to host the national team. After Celtic were chosen as hosts for England's four previous visits, Rangers' directors sanctioned over £20,000 of improvement works to be made to Ibrox. In 1902 the major investment was rewarded with the awarding of the Home Championship match between England and Scotland.[40]

Come 5 April 1902, Scotland were hosting England not just for bragging rights but also with the title at stake. England needed the win to topple Scotland, and Ibrox was packed with a reported 65,000–70,000 spectators. The West Tribune Stand was such a squeeze that historian Robert Sheils described the supporters as having space of just 16 inches by 14 inches![41] Half an hour into the game on that April afternoon is when disaster struck the footballing world: joints underneath the stands gave way and the wooden boardings fell through. Early reports, including *The Scotsman* from the Monday following, claimed 18 people died with 200 others injured, as a 'seething crowd of humanity' horrifically fell over 40 feet to the ground below.[42] However, these numbers were thought to later total at 25 deaths and over 500 injuries of ranging severity.

Unbelievably, with the hospitals in Glasgow full of casualties and police cells now being used as medical holding bays, the match still resumed that day – the 1-1 scoreline later being voided. Players were said to be traumatised, with reports of match shirts being used as bandages, but officials feared worse injuries by abandoning the tie. In the aftermath of the disaster, the FA donated £500 to a relief fund for the victims of that terrible day and both football associations agreed to a replay at Villa Park on 3 May 1902. This game would finish

40   *The Telegraph*, 30 December 2010

41   Shiels, R. (1998) 'The Fatalities at the Ibrox Disaster of 1902', *The Sports Historian*, 18(2), pp.148-55

42   *The Scotsman*, 7 April 1902

2-2, handing the British Home Championship to Scotland, but more importantly it united the footballing world with proceeds from the game also being donated to the fund. Legal proceedings would follow, as the supplier of the pine for the terrace joists was charged with 'culpable homicide' but was later acquitted.[43] The impact of this tragedy saw stadiums that had similar combined wooden/steel terracing changed. Rangers immediately rebuilt parts of Ibrox, with other British clubs following suit too.

The Home Championships would see attendance figures generally remain the same, but the next time Scotland met England north of the border, the number of fans reached only 45,000 at Celtic Park. The tragedy at Ibrox had left a scar in the, up-to-then, impeccable Scottish football records. Scotland wouldn't win the championship outright again until 1910, an eight-year gap which was comfortably the longest in their history.

History would repeat itself 69 years later as another disaster struck Ibrox in 1971. The incident was not caused by the stadium's structure, but by a crush of supporters leaving the ground through an exit stairway. Following an Old Firm clash, the large number of fans present at the ground meant the resulting death count of 66 was the highest in British sport at the time. Such neglect for fan safety, particularly with regards to football stadia, would sadly recur throughout football's history. As moments 12, 29 and 32 will further explain, lessons would continue to be learnt, but shockingly at the expense of hundreds of supporters across the country.

8

FIFA Founded (1904)

On 21 May 1904 the Fédération Internationale de Football Association (FIFA) was founded in Paris. Love them or loathe them today, FIFA have been integral to the growth and globalisation of the 'beautiful game'. FIFA's founding was a way of formalising, across the world, the work begun by the Football Association back in 1863. This was then followed by the first-ever international football match held at Hamilton Crescent, Glasgow, between Scotland and England in 1872 (Moment 4).

By 1904, there was a European hunger for coordination of football; however, the home nations of England, Scotland, Ireland and Wales rejected the idea. Holt describes the English attitude as 'proud and insular'[44], refusing to join the new federation, despite FIFA's own admission that Netherlands FA secretary Carl Hirschman had approached the English FA's secretary, FJ Wall, to help lead the new organisation.[45] When Scotland, Ireland and Wales followed England's lead to protect their game from foreign influence, the prospective new European association was dealt a blow.

---

44 Richard Holt, *Sport and the British* (Oxford: Oxford University Press, 1989) p.273

45 FIFA Website, 'History of FIFA – Foundation', *FIFA*, https://www.fifa.com/about-fifa/who-we-are/history/index.html

However, despite these disappointing rejections, many national associations did agree to unite together. In total seven countries founded FIFA in May 1904: France, Netherlands, Belgium, Spain, Sweden, Denmark and Switzerland were at the meeting whilst Germany also joined from afar by telegram. Robert Guérin, a French journalist for *Le Matin* newspaper, was elected the first president of FIFA. The decision was reported in British newspapers, *The Sportsman* commenting that 'the new Federation is bound to play an important part in the future'[46] of football – how right they were!

It was decided by September 1905 (after England had finally joined) that matches were to be played according to the 'Laws of the Game of the Football Association Ltd'.[47] Each national association would also pay an annual membership fee of 50 French francs. Significantly, only FIFA could organise official international matches and so their influence began to grow further. By the beginning of the First World War in 1914, many more had joined the fray, with South Africa, Canada, USA, Argentina and Chile making FIFA truly global. It would not be until 1930, though, that the first World Cup would take place, but that is for a future moment (13).

Today, FIFA's reach is of course immense. Its motto of 'For the Game. For the World' has seen football spread across the globe, with 211 national associations members of the organisation. The World Cup has been hosted 21 times in 17 different countries, on five different continents – eight different nations (in their current form) lifting the glorious title.[48] In 2022 Qatar will play host to a winter World Cup. The controversial decision to hand it to the state has been questioned, scrutinised and investigated, but it does undoubtedly show a desire to spread the beautiful game far and wide.

46 *The Sportsman*, 23 June 1904
47 FIFA Website, 'History of FIFA – Foundation'
48 *Ibid*

FIFA now hosts tournaments for both men's and women's football in Under-17, Under-20, Senior and Olympic categories. In recent years this has expanded into more modern areas, such as the FIFA Futsal World Cup, the FIFA Beach Soccer World Cup and even the FIFA eWorld Cup (for video gamers). 21 May 1904, though, will remain ingrained in the history of the game as the day the march towards global integration of football began.

9

Billy Meredith and the Founding of the AFPTU (1907)

William (Billy) Meredith was born in Chirk, Denbighshire, North Wales, in 1874. He followed the village profession of mining and at just the age of 12 took a job at the local colliery. Football, though, was Meredith's true love, a game that had swept the working classes and offered an escape from the harsh reality of pit life. Meredith represented English clubs Northwich Victoria and Ardwick AFC (who became Manchester City) as an amateur, whilst still mining, before later turning professional.

Football at this time was still adjusting to the professional game and a maximum wage cap had been introduced. £4-a-week was set in 1900/01 and this could not be broken to match talent, experience or the desire of another club to attract a player. The Association Footballers' Union (AFU) had been founded in 1898 to negotiate with the FA on behalf of players, but this was dissolved in 1901, leaving footballers with no representation. Meredith, perhaps inspired by the mining community of his home town, set about wishing to organise a union to represent the interests of these professional sportsmen 'owned' by their clubs.

Holt records that 'around two million spectators' attended Football League matches in the mid-1890s, and by the 1905/06 campaign this figure had 'shot up to six million'.[49] Meredith and other professional footballers believed they should be paid a fair wage for the weekly entertainment they were providing the millions of supporters. As Butler puts it, 'players all over the country were increasingly aware of their worth' as the wage cap became the biggest issue facing British football.[50]

On 2 December 1907, Meredith (now of Manchester United) and his team-mate Charlie Roberts formed the *Association of Football Players' and Trainers' Union* (the AFPTU, and forerunner of the PFA). The meeting, held at Manchester's Imperial Hotel, was reportedly done with 'great harmony' as a committee was elected to run the union.[51] The AFPTU targeted changes to the maximum wage cap and transfer regulations that saw players severely restricted in club movement.

The issue of money had been long debated by football administrators, and the Football Association's agreement to back professionalism had only come with the promise of their ultimate financial control. With Meredith and his supporters arguing for greater financial investment in players from their clubs, there was genuine concern that this would hand power to the Football League and away from the FA if the Football League continued to back the idea of paying 'win bonuses' to supplement players' wages.

In 1909, at an FA members' meeting with issues coming to a head, Mr Sydney (representing Wolverhampton Wanderers) remarked of the 'evil of bonuses' offered to players to win games, and that 'if they were paid, the game would degenerate into a prize fight'. To Mr Sydney, 'bonuses in the past had been the cause of all the evil in football, and payments as suggested would be certain to lead to corruption'.[52] The attitude of the

---

49   Richard Holt, *Sport and the British*, p.161

50   Bryon Butler, *The Football League: The First 100 Years* (Guildford: Colour Library Books Ltd., 1988), p.32

51   *Sporting Life*, 3 December 1907

52   *Sheffield Daily Telegraph*, 10 June 1909

FA towards greater financial freedom for players did not bode well for Meredith and the AFPTU.

The decision of the AFPTU's leaders to unite with the Federation of Trade Unions (who became the Trades Union Congress) in 1909 disgusted both the Football League and the FA. So much so, that the latter withdrew recognition of AFPTU and many players involved faced banishment from the game. The players responded by threatening strikes but this caused public support to ebb away and clubs held firm too, lining up amateurs to take the striking players' places.[53] The threat of strikes was averted but change was coming.

Meredith and his comrades stood firm, and eventually some concession was implemented by the FA. In 1910 'Rule 31' was adjusted, allowing players to be paid extra bonuses as part of their contracts by clubs. However, 'Rule 30', the maximum wage, would remain, with transfer regulations still kept tight.[54] Whilst much higher than the best wages in the job market for other skilled labourers, the new £5-a-week limit was still not given to the majority of players, meaning many professionals were underpaid.[55] Despite Billy Meredith's war not being successful during his playing days, the Wales, Man City and Man United legend on the pitch is also owed a lot for his fight for players' rights off it too. The PFA (who followed on from the AFPTU) still exist to this day, standing up for the players they represent. A later moment, meanwhile, will see Meredith's ambitions come to fruition in 1961 (Moment 21).

53 John Williams, *Reds: Liverpool Football Club – The Biography* (London, Random House, 2011)

54 *Ibid*

55 Richard Holt, *Sport and The British*, p.293

10

The Christmas Truce and the Footballers' Battalions (1914–18)

When Archduke Franz Ferdinand, heir to the Austro-Hungarian throne, was assassinated in Sarajevo on 28 June 1914, little did Europe know that it would lead to over four years of brutal bloodshed. The First World War saw an estimated 11 million soldiers lose their lives from over 30 countries across the world. The Great War, as it was known, had a major impact on every aspect of life, meaning sport was of course affected.

Initially, football would continue into the 1914/15 campaign; however, this led to many calling football 'unpatriotic' for continuing whilst men were fighting and dying at war. The motion to suspend football was debated in Parliament, Liberal MP James Hogge asking, 'In view of the gravity of the crisis and the need for recruits, will he [the Prime Minister] introduce legislation taking powers to suppress all professional football matches during the continuance of the War?'[56] At the end of 1914/15, football was indeed suspended and fighting-fit footballers were encouraged to sign up to join the armed forces.

---

56 House of Commons, *Hansard's Parliamentary Debates: The Official Report* (26 November 1914, vol. 68) http://hansard.parliament.uk/commons

Before football was postponed, the sport was involved in the war in the Christmas of 1914. 'The Christmas truce' is perhaps one of the most well-known stories about the First World War. It was an unbelievable moment of peace and normality during 'the war to end all wars'. The accuracy of the story has, of course, been debated over the years, but the beautiful game's involvement is what makes it so significant.

On Christmas Eve 1914, months into a war that was supposed to last 'until Christmas', it was clear there was no end in sight. The tale goes that the Germans began singing carols, and the British then responded with some of their own. Suddenly, in the horrors of war, human beings decided to set aside their weapons for Christmas Day. Officers were said to be unhappy at this unarranged ceasefire up and down the Western Front (although not everywhere did experience this). Football matches reportedly broke out too, as soldiers reclaimed what they were missing, the Allies v the Central Powers ... there was no winter break in the trenches that year!

The *Chester Chronicle* provides an eye-witness account of the truce from one soldier:

'Then the strangest thing happened. As if by some mutual agreement, both sides clambered out of the trenches, and met in the middle of the field. We exchanged cigarettes etc., and had general conversation. One of them came up to officer and said in broken English: "Good morning sir; I live at Alexander Road, Horusey, and I would see Woolwich Arsenal play Tottenham tomorrow."' [57]

Some historians, including Taff Gillingham, have debated the nature of the Christmas truce. He calls the story 'romanticised', as he concedes that 'there were 44 infantry battalions that did take part in the truce in some way or another, but they didn't all get out of the trenches'. Despite this scepticism, he believes 'up to 30,000 men got out of the trenches and met the Germans', adding that 'only 20 or

---

57 *Chester Chronicle*, 9 January 1915

absolutely maximum 30 may have kicked a football about'.[58] This may not fit with the common public remembrance of the truce, but it does show that the love of the beautiful game was present in the horrors of war.

Dr Iain Adams has also researched the event, writing that 'in some places I have no doubt at all that they played football but it was not a football match'. What perhaps is far more likely is that some began 'kicking a can about', before a football-mad soldier pulled out his ball brought from home. So, 'in two or three places a real football would have been used'[59] and these incidents have led to the famous story of the Christmas truce we have today.

Christmas football match or not on that day in 1914, one piece of history that is not up for debate is the importance the 'pals battalions' played in war-time recruitment. The British government, to increase recruitment and volunteers, set up these 'pals battalions' to encourage men to sign up for the war with their friends, a clever tactic. Hundreds were formed across the UK and within these were football clubs, who saw service as a duty far greater than continuing the sport.

Walter Tull, Northampton Town (and former Tottenham Hotspur) half-back was one of those to sign up (even before football was suspended). Tull's significance is even greater, in that he was one of the first black players to play in England. Alongside this, he became one of Britain's first-ever black army officers. Sadly, Tull lost his life (aged 29) on 23 March 1918, leading his men into action at a battle near Favreuil, France.[60] What a man!

The 17th Battalion, Middlesex Regiment, became the first 'football battalion' and was followed by 23rd Battalion, Middlesex Regiment. These two units both served valiantly

---

58 *The Telegraph*, 25 December 2014

59 *Ibid*

60 Richard Conway and David Lockwood, 'Walter Tull: The incredible story of a football pioneer and war hero', *BBC Sport* (23 March 1918) https://www.bbc.co.uk/sport/football/43504448

at the infamous Battle of the Somme in 1916, and of the 600 original men who formed the 17th Battalion, a staggering 500 are estimated to have lost their lives. Hundreds of thousands of football-mad men from up and down Britain were killed during the Great War. Football was truly changed by a generation who fought for freedom, yet sacrificed not just their careers but their lives too.

1917–49

11

Women's Football in
World War One (1917–21)

The First World War was a conflict like no other. Throughout history there have been numerous struggles between nations, but never to the scale seen between 1914 and 1918. Being a total war, it required each and everyone in society to play their part. For women, the front line wasn't an option. Rather, most were required to help fill the void left by men in munitions factories across the nation. Munitions were key to the war effort as wave after wave of shells were fired across no-man's land and towards the enemy. In an era when women's calls for suffrage had been repeatedly cast to one side, it was a selfless act by many.

As the war progressed, the number of fallen continued to rise – even as high as 60,000 on the first day of the Somme offensive in 1916. Unsurprisingly, domestic morale was low – leading to a group of ladies doing something truly remarkable. A team was set up at the Dick, Kerr munitions factory in Preston. Pioneered by Grace Sibbert, a factory worker, and Alfred Frankland, her colleague, they had seen women beating the male co-workers in kickabouts during tea and lunch breaks.[61]

---

61   Barbara Jacobs, *The Dick, Kerr's Ladies* (London: Constable and Robinson, 2004)

The first match of the Dick, Kerr Ladies took place in Preston on Christmas Day 1917 in front of a reported 10,000 spectators. Despite now being regarded as the most popular and most successful of the ladies' sides, women's football matches had taken place in the months prior to Sibbert and Frankland's side's first appearance.[62] Indeed, what becomes clear is that a genuine female football movement was beginning to take shape. The primary concern of those playing was to increase morale, but the talent on display in the growing number of teams meant the novelty of 'women playing football' soon wore off.

Now it became about the quality of football and teams would develop their own 'fanatical' supporters.[63] Of course, that is not to say that women's football was totally immune to misogynistic calls from the touchline, but growing crowds suggested that these were in the minority.

The popularity of women's football didn't fade after the armistice in 1918. Indeed, the Dick, Kerr Ladies in particular began to attract large crowds at stadiums after the war. This included a staggering 53,000 at Goodison Park on Boxing Day 1920.[64] The team was so popular that once the Football League had returned, the Dick, Kerr Ladies were still drawing larger attendances, much to the FA's dismay. In 1921 the association would pass a draconian piece of legislation banning women from playing on FA affiliated grounds.

The ban would come as a shock to many, but was widely welcomed by a misogynistic majority. Newspapers were quick in their condemnation of the women's game. Describing it as a novelty and a 'burlesque', the same papers which had praised women's football in the First World War were now actively discouraging it.[65] Furthermore, public opinion was also

---

62 Jean Williams, *A Beautiful Game: International Perspectives on Women's Football* (Oxford: Berg, 2007)

63 Barbara Jacobs, *The Dick, Kerr's Ladies*

64 *Lancashire Evening Post*, 28 December 1920

65 *Yorkshire Evening Post*, 6 December 1921

staunchly against the game. In a scathing attack from Bishop Welldon, he believes those playing to merely be 'imitators of men'.[66] Even in the knowledge that charities, like those of ex-servicemen, would miss out on a great deal of donations, opinions were firmly set to prohibit the playing of women's football. In December 1921 it was banned.

Counter-opinions can be found, but are in far shorter supply. The *Lancashire Evening Post* featured an article in which it drew attention to the charity work from the players. Praising this endeavour, it also makes note of the fact that women's football players never expected to make personal profit out of the game, although the writer believes they probably should.[67] A quite incredible article written by a 'female correspondent' in the Welsh *Western Mail* delivers an impassioned defence of women and their right to play sports. She cites the original opposition to such sports as cycling, lawn tennis, lacrosse and hockey before explaining how public perception has changed over time. Indeed, this could become the case with football. Calls of 'over-exertion' being the main reason for the ban are dismissed as a mere side-effect of sport.[68]

This drastic resolution didn't fully stop the women's teams, however. After 1921 friendlies still took place and international tours were arranged. Striker Lily Parr was the superstar of the Dick, Kerr Ladies and would retire decades later after scoring over 900 goals. Although never reaching the heights of wartime, the movement is surely one of the game's most important. It gave women a platform and a voice in a time when both had seemed so alien to many. In 1918 women finally achieved the vote and it seems that football played a big part in making this possible.

Today, the study of women's football in the First World War has boomed. The modern growth of the game has led to

---

66 *Sheffield Independent*, 19 December 1921

67 *Lancashire Evening Post*, 6 December 1921

68 *Western Mail*, 10 December 1921

greater interest and efforts being dedicated to the broadening of people's knowledge on the topic. With an increasing number of female role models like Megan Rapinoe, Alex Morgan and Ada Hegerberg, the history of women's football is likely to receive an incredible boost. The recent World Cup Final between the USA and the Netherlands attracted almost 58,000 supporters, further demonstrating that for the women's game the only way is up.

12

The White Horse Final (1923)

Football had been taken to the hearts and minds of the public like no other sport. In its first 60 years it had grown rapidly into the most popular game around the world. The rise of professionalism and the growth of major clubs in the north and south of Britain had seen average attendances in the First Division rise to over 27,000 in 1922. By 1923 the FA Cup had become the biggest competition in sport, with hundreds of professional and amateur teams entering. The popularity of the competition had led to the final that year being played, for the first time, at Wembley Stadium.

Then called the Empire Stadium, its capacity of 127,000 far outnumbered the previous venue for the FA Cup Final – Stamford Bridge. With a maximum attendance of just over 80,000 fans, the West London ground was never going to provide a permanent home for English football. Indeed, prior to the outbreak of the First World War, over 120,000 people had crammed into Crystal Palace to watch Aston Villa defeat Sunderland 1-0. There was clearly an appetite for mass spectatorship. What Wembley offered was state-of-the-art engineering and a chance for everyone to see the action.[69]

69   Richard William Cox, et al, *Encyclopaedia of British Football* (London: Frank Cass, 2002)

The 1923 final saw Bolton Wanderers face off against London side West Ham United. Under the eyes of King George V, officially 126,047 supporters attended the game. However, wider reports and images from the day show that potentially 300,000 fans filed into the stadium, eventually spilling onto the pitch. Attempting to restore order, the police began to shepherd the fans back to the terraces. Although one of many mounted police helping to get the game underway, the image of a white horse in between thousands of fans has defined the match. Although debated, the good behaviour of the crowd on the day was perhaps to thank for there being no fatalities, but 1,000 people did suffer injuries.

Recent studies have attributed the calming down of the crowd to the arrival of King George V. For many, the arrival of royalty and the subsequent playing of the national anthem gave the crowd something to focus on. Indeed, tens of thousands of fans who had moved in the direction of the royal box were eventually shepherded out of the ground, clearing space for the match to commence.[70]

For many, the final was indeed a fiasco. The mass attendance and the inability of organisers to let only ticket holders in, prompted parliamentary debate on the issue. Unsurprisingly, although discussed, little was actually done. The entrances to the stadium were picked up as a problem, before George Buchanan put forward the suggestion that future FA Cup Finals should be played in Glasgow so 'it may be properly conducted'. Infamous politician Oswald Mosley was quick to describe the actions of fans at the match as hooliganism before being shot down by Jack Jones. Jones had reiterated that those present were good-humoured and that suggestions of hooliganism were not right.[71]

Ultimately, the game was not deemed worthy enough for government regulation, unlike other cultural pastimes, the

---

70 Jeff Hill, *Soccer and Disaster* (London: Routledge, 2005) p.35

71 House of Commons, *Hansard's Parliamentary Debates: The Official Report* (30 April 1923, vol. 163) http://hansard.parliament.uk/commons

music hall and theatre.[72] Such beliefs meant that regulation into football stadia, at least in Britain, would struggle to make any real inroads. Furthermore, the event helped to add to the narrative of the well-behaved Brit. It showed English fans to be self-disciplined and only needing the firm hand of a single policeman to regain control.[73] Indeed, during the same parliamentary debate, praise was heaped upon the rider of the white horse and the police in general.

The importance of this moment is in itself – the sheer amount of spectators shows us the popularity of football and its influence on the masses. Like nothing else in society, the beautiful game offered identity and allegiance. It is a notion which is still seen today as thousands pour into stadia around the world. A vital lesson to be drawn from the White Horse Final is what *didn't* happen as a result. The negligence shown would bring with it disastrous consequences towards the end of the 20th century. The legacy of the White Horse still remains with the naming of a bridge towards the new Wembley dedicated to its legend. What of the rider? Constable Scorey was given free tickets to future cup finals, but unfortunately he wasn't a football fan so failed to attend!

72   Matthew Taylor, *The Association Game* (London: Routledge, 2008)
73   Jeff Hill, *Soccer and Disaster* (London: Routledge, 2005) p.36

13

The First FIFA World Cup (1930)

In the modern game, there is a quadrennial event which excites each and every football fan: the FIFA World Cup. In 1930 the tournament was born, with Uruguay becoming the inaugural hosts. Thirteen teams from around the world would head to South America in order to reveal who was the greatest footballing nation on Earth. Perhaps what is most perplexing when looking into the first countries to participate is the lack of the 'home nations'. It is no secret that England, Scotland, Wales and Ireland were the first international sides in existence, so why weren't they in Uruguay?

Following its success in covering the United Kingdom, football's next biggest players were in South America. Although introduced to the game by the British c.1900, it hadn't taken long for a distinct South American footballing identity to emerge.[74] High attendances at early matches, particularly against invitees from England, showed the game was already immensely popular. The game had reached the height of popularity across the Atlantic and by 1916 CONMEBOL (South American football's governing body) was established. Originally proposed as a confederation between the nations of the River

---

74 Tony Mason, *Passion of the People?: Football in South America* (London: Verso, 1995) p.23

Plate (Argentina and Uruguay), Brazil and Chile would join the institution.[75] Following a successful inaugural tournament to mark the founding of CONMEBOL, the game would continue to grow and proof of successful tournament football would prompt wider calls for a greater competition.

The first 'Copa America' had proven to be football's first international tournament, but it was the success of the 1924 and 1928 Olympic football tournaments which really instigated a FIFA meeting to discuss the chance of a world football championships. In 1930 this vision became a reality. As double Olympic gold medallists, it seemed fitting that Uruguay would host the first edition of the tournament. Despite South American support, the awarding of the competition to Uruguay would lead to widespread bitterness from European nations.[76]

The home nations believed the 'World Cup' to be beneath them. The relationship between the FA and FIFA had always been strained, ever since the latter's formation in 1904. English football would remain 'insular', with a much greater focus on the league than the national team. The reluctance was found even greater under the notion that football was 'Britain's game' and that there was no need to cooperate with the wider continent.[77] For the rest of the home nations, the annual championship played across England, Scotland, Wales and Ireland was of a far higher standard anyway.

Despite a general European boycott, four teams did accept an invitation to compete. FIFA, by 1930, had grown considerably but faced doubt over its future due to the animosity between nations following the First World War. The home nations had withdrawn from the organisation and, although invited to take part, cited the long travel distances

---

75   *Ibid*, p.30

76   Clemente A. Lisi, *A History of the World Cup* (Plymouth: Scarecrow, 2011) p.9

77   Richard Holt, *Sport and the British*, p.273

and an unwillingness to play against wartime enemies as a reason not to travel to Uruguay.[78]

So what of the first World Cup? How did events unfold? Following play in the four groups (three groups of three and one group of four), the winners of each progressed to the semi-final stage. Joining the hosts in the last four were neighbours Argentina, Yugoslavia and, perhaps surprisingly, the USA. What became clear when play was kicked off in the two semi-finals was the gulf in class between Uruguay, Argentina and their opponents. With both sides winning 6-1 in front of capacity crowds at the newly built Estadio Centenario, the final was sure to be a classic.

The final itself was initially disrupted by a dispute over who would provide the match ball. The final decision was for Argentina to use their ball in the first half, with the Uruguayans playing with theirs after the break. What is apparent from various reports of the final is the tribal atmosphere it created. Football was truly more than just what happened over 90 minutes. It was a source of identity.

Uruguay eventually emerged victorious, winning 4-2 after an exhilarating 90 minutes. Despite heading into half-time 2-1 down, a strong second half saw 'La Celeste', roared on by a partisan crowd, score three goals to turn the match around. Amazingly, the final goal was scored by Hector Castro, a player who at the age of 13 had his forearm accidentally amputated. Captain Jose Nasazzi would lift the Jules Rimet trophy for the first time and write his nation's name into football history.

The inaugural tournament's success has been debated ever since. Over 68,000 spectators watched the final, which showed football's immense power and influence around the globe. Success meant the tournament would continue every four years, starting in Italy in 1934. On the other hand, the lack of strong European sides and the home nations meant the tournament was arguably not an accurate representation

---

78   *Ibid*, p.10

of the best in world football. What has stood the test of time is the legacy of the tournament. With it still being the world's most popular and most watched sporting spectacle, the steps taken in Uruguay will live long in the memory of football fans around the globe.

14

The First Televised
Football Match (1937)

Today, football and television go hand-in-hand. It is a relationship which causes controversy and debate, but in 1937 the first televised match would truly change the game forever. The leading figure in broadcasting throughout the 1930s had been the BBC. The corporation had been growing rapidly ever since its founding in 1926 and radio broadcasts of football matches offered some of the most popular shows on the 'wireless'. Cardiff City's historic victory over Arsenal at Wembley had been the first to have live radio coverage. The broadcast had been popular with fans, particularly in Cardiff, as large speakers were erected in the city centre.[79]

Before the final, Liverpool had already banned the BBC from broadcasting a league game with Newcastle in February. Citing a lack of knowledge around the success of such practices, they didn't 'feel disposed to allow it'.[80] Following the final, the seemingly well-liked radio broadcast meant that, within weeks, questions as to the frequency of such transmissions were raised. Indeed, some leading Football League clubs were immediately opposed to the idea. There was a genuine fear

---

79 Huggins, Mike (2007) BBC radio and sport 1922–39. *Contemporary British History*, 21 (4). pp.491-515

80 *Nottingham Evening Post*, 11 February 1927

for 'gates' at league grounds. The *Birmingham Daily Gazette* foresaw a fall of around 10,000 people if results were broadcast on the BBC.[81] Such estimates were unfounded, but did little to halt the anxiety towards new technology.

In allowing coverage of the FA Cup Final and other 'national' events like Wimbledon and the Boat Race, the BBC saw it as an opportunity to cement its place as the nation's platform for cultural pastimes and events.[82] By the mid-1930s, radio had firmly found its place in football coverage and gate receipts had not seen much loss. In 1937, however, the rapid advancement in television brought into question the suitability of a new kind of broadcast. Once again, the footballing world would be divided, and technology was at its centre.

Specially arranged for the occasion, the first match to be televised was between Arsenal and Arsenal Reserves. According to *The Era*, three cameras were to be used, one in the stands and a further two behind the goals to give a 'comprehensive view of the ground … and close ups of the players'.[83] Unfortunately for anyone watching, bad light affected the coverage as rain and dark clouds loomed overhead.[84] Perhaps this explains the lack of newspaper coverage following the event. The experiment did help to enthuse the curiosity of many and, despite lacking initial response, its long-term legacy is incredible.

The main reason for a lack of media coverage is that the match at Highbury was not broadcast to the general public. Indeed, the game was watched internally, with its main goal being to answer questions about the functionality of such a practice. Within a year of the test transmission, further matches had been arranged by the BBC to be televised to the wider British public.

---

81 *Birmingham Daily Gazette*, 17 August 1928
82 Roger Domeneghetti, *From the Back Page to the Front Room* (Glasgow: Ockley, 2017)
83 *The Era*, 9 September 1937
84 *Hartlepool Daily Mail*, 17 September 1937

The BBC had battled for permission to broadcast frequent league fixtures, but to no avail. The FA permitted two ties to be shown, however, in September 1938. The first saw Arsenal once again as they took on Preston North End, before an exhibition match between England and the Rest of Europe was shown a month later.[85]

Drawing striking comparisons to modern-day football, the debate would continue into 1939 as worries over revenue and a 'fear of innovation' took to the forefront of many supporters' minds.[86] Furthermore, league sides were reluctant to allow televised matches, with both Wolverhampton Wanderers and Portsmouth letting their opinions known before the 1939 FA Cup Final. The final itself was broadcast by the BBC.[87]

Worries over gate receipts were unfounded. Previous fears that attendance numbers would fall by up to 10,000 did not come to fruition. Perhaps surprisingly, average numbers recorded at top-flight grounds actually went up from 24,605 in 1937 to 25,160 the following year. The same trend was seen across the lower leagues as numbers increased. Television, like radio ten years earlier, seemed to benefit more from the wider coverage and new audiences it attracted to games.

The Second World War would see the Football League suspended just three games in as players were once more called upon to aid the war effort. Although difficult to regard as 'mass media' in 1939, television would eventually have the power to transform the representation and economics of sport.[88] We will see this in greater depth in moment 35. Today, it is common to see the news dominated by football and television rights. It is possible now to watch football all day if we wanted on a multitude of channels as the commercialisation of the game

---

85 *Birmingham Daily Gazette*, 30 August 1938

86 *Dundee Evening Telegraph*, 5 June 1939

87 *Liverpool Daily Post*, 5 April 1939

88 Mike Huggins, *Sport and the English: 1918–1939* (London: Routledge, 2006) p.41

continues. What needs reminding, though, is in 1937 the beauty of the game was truly captured and taken to the hearts of those who watched it – let's hope that feeling returns.

15

Superga Air Disaster (1949)

Despite being less than 100 years old, football and its growing number of worldwide supporters had seen many beautiful moments. In 1949, however, it was to see one of its darkest. Since the turn of the century, Italian football or *calcio* grew into one of the sport's most celebrated forms of the game. Following two successive World Cup victories in the 1930s, the nation boasted some of the game's finest players. Giuseppe Meazza had been the star of the show for Vittorio Pozzo's all-conquering heroes before a new star featured in the following decade, Valentino Mazzola.

Mazzola was playing for northern Italian giants Torino. Due to their superiority in domestic competition, they became known as the 'Grande Torino'. What was most impressive was their early success. Despite the ongoing Second World War, the side had quickly become the dominant team in the country. Winning the *Scudetto* in 1943, the side were the final champions before the league was suspended. An allied invasion of the south had meant the league would disband for the final years of the Second World War. Following the conflict's end in 1945, the Italian league restarted with Torino playing in a 'Northern Italy Serie A'.

Torino would emerge victorious ahead of Inter and Juventus and thus qualified for a final-eight team tournament alongside clubs from the centre and south of Italy. The side's perfect home record saw them crowned champions by a single point. Scoring 43 goals in just 14 games, the prowess of the side was unquestionable. A season later, Torino would win the unified Serie A by ten points, scoring over 100 goals. The feat seemed unique, but the following year saw a 15-point gap between Torino and runners-up Milan; 125 goals had been scored, with Mazzola scoring 25. The side featured heavily in the national team. During a friendly against an emerging Hungary, Torino players filled ten out of the 11 positions.[89]

The 'Grande Torino' came to represent more than just the locality of Turin. Indeed, their success and dominance was a cause for national pride. Following the years of devastation that had rocked the Italian peninsula to its very core, a side showing such teamwork, skill and togetherness became a cause for celebration.[90] Italy had been on the losing side of the Second World War and their place on the world stage was under intense scrutiny, but having such a team would truly help to represent more than just the 11 on the pitch. Such was Torino's fame, they became one of the first Italian sides to play friendlies abroad.

In May 1949, following a friendly match in Lisbon against Portuguese side Benfica, the side and coaching staff returned to Turin by plane. Poor visibility and malfunctioning equipment meant the plane would struggle to see through the weather.[91] Out of nowhere, the Superga Basilica, sat on top of a hill, appeared in front of the pilots who had no time to react. The resulting crash claimed the lives of all 31 people on board. A squad was killed and a footballing superpower was stopped tragically in its prime.

---

89   Paul Dietschy, 'The Superga Disaster and the Death of the Great Torino', *Soccer and Disaster* (London: Routledge, 2005)

90   'Italian Football Tragedy Still Emotional', *FIFATV* https://www.youtube.com/watch?v=9bNsGzhkXOg

91   Patrick Jennings, 'The Plane Crash that Killed Serie A's Champions and their English Coach', *BBC Sport* (4 May 2019)

The disaster sent shockwaves around the footballing world. In the immediate aftermath, the whole of Italy was brought together in national mourning.[92] Over half a million people would attend the funeral held two days later for the players, coaches and journalists who died. As far as South America, the date of the disaster was to be remembered through days of football in the coming years.[93] For the remainder of the league season, Torino played their youth team as the Italian FA agreed to award the title to the side as a mark of respect.

Italian football was left in tatters, with many believing the disaster put *calcio* back 30 years.[94] The international team which had relied so heavily on the Torino players was left empty. The resulting World Cup in Brazil had left the Italy squad reluctant to fly to South America. Indeed, the team would travel two weeks by ship to reach the finals. A swift first-round exit further compounded the nation's misery. Subsequent World Cups were also met with early departures as Italian football took 20 years to truly recuperate.

The legacy of Superga is still strongly felt today. Torino would struggle to recover in the years following the event and have arguably never reached the achievements set by Mazzola and co. What sets the moment apart is the question of 'what could have been?' Torino were, in 1949, a side creating history with each and every game they played and they are, without a doubt, one of football's greatest ever teams. The side had come to reflect the rejuvenation and reconstruction of Italy and people across the country could see hope again. Despite the millions of deaths in World War Two, it would be the 31 in May 1949 that truly brought the nation together.

---

92   Paddy Agnew, *Forza Italia: The Fall and Rise of Italian Football* (Ebury, 2007) p.60

93   Paul Dietschy, *Superga Disaster*, p.175

94   John Foot, *Calcio: A History of Italian Football* (London: Harper Perennial, 2007) p.94

1950–60

16

The 1950 FIFA World Cup (1950)

The 1950 FIFA World Cup is truly one of football's greatest-ever moments, and in many ways one to be considered as the beginning of football's 'modern' era. Following the Second World War (1939–45), many countries across the world were recovering and getting back on their feet. In Britain, the NHS had been founded by the post-war Labour government, which promised free healthcare for all at the point of use; however, some of the wartime hangovers still existed. The 1948 Olympic Games were held in London on a 'tiny budget', dubbed the 'Austerity' Olympics.[95] These Olympics were so successful that it was hoped the first post-war World Cup in 1950 would help to bring countries together after two cancelled editions in 1942 and 1946, the former touted to be hosted in Nazi Germany before war broke out.

Brazil would be chosen as the host in 1950, the tournament taking place in South America rather than war-torn Europe. This would also please the South American countries who demanded the competition be rotated between Europe and the Americas following Italy 1934 and France 1938. The Jules Rimet trophy itself would have to be dug out of its wartime hiding place, a shoebox under the bed of FIFA vice-president

---

95   Janie Hampton, *The Austerity Olympics: When the Games Came to London in 1948* (London: Aurum Press Limited, 2008) p.3

Ottorino Barassi, where it was kept safe from Nazi hands.[96] The tournament originally had 16 registered to compete but only 12 made the journey to Brazil as India, Turkey, France and Scotland all withdrew. Notably, though, the World Cup would finally see a first appearance for a home nations side, England. The English had refused to enter in 1930, 1934 or 1938, not wishing to put their self-proclaimed status of 'greatness' on the line with other nations.

England, along with the other home nations, had long been the team to beat. Considered the fathers of the sport, they would be the scalp all sides wanted to take. England were drawn in the same group as the USA, Chile and Spain, England beating Chile 2-0 in their opener. Next up were the USA – what threat would they pose? None – was certainly the general consensus! So on 29 June 1950, at the Estadio Independencia in Belo Horizonte, in front of 10,000+ spectators, the stage was set for Walter Winterbottom's England to waltz past the part-timers of the USA. USA's Scottish-born coach, Bill Jeffrey, had only been appointed two weeks before the World Cup and summed up the feelings pre-game: 'We have no chance ... [we are] sheep ready to be slaughtered'.[97]

There is a familiar ring to England losing as favourites at a major tournament, and 1950 is another of those cases. The English dominated the early stages of the tie, US keeper Frank Borghi making plenty of saves to keep it goalless. Then, in the 37th minute, a long range effort from US midfielder Walter Bahr was deflected into the back of the net by a diving header from forward and part-time dishwasher Joe Gaetjens. The crowd was sent into raptures, the 'Miracle on Grass' had occurred! The USA held on to their lead to win 1-0 and England were left stunned.

---

96 Clemente A. Lisi, *A History of the World Cup* (Plymouth: Scarecrow Press, INC., 2011) p.44

97 Michael Grant and Rob Robertson, *The Management: Scotland's Great Football Bosses* (Edinburgh: Birlinn, 2011)

The game was such a shock that not a single American newspaper had even sent a journalist to cover the match. In Britain, the reports that filtered through stunned many. Some newspapers even believed the scoreline was a mistake and printed it either as 10-1 or 10-0 to England.[98] When the papers did get it right they were scathing. The *Birmingham Daily Gazette* called it 'A black day for England',[99] whilst the *Nottingham Evening Post* called it an 'Unbelievable defeat'.[100] To make matters worse, England would then lose to Spain three days later and be dumped out of their first World Cup. England were not the kings of football ... It was a big wake-up call!

This was not the sole jaw-dropper of 1950. To those who adore the South American game, *'Maracanazo'*, or 'The Agony of Maracanã', is a strand that continues to run through football on that continent to this day. Hosts Brazil had run riot during their home World Cup, remaining unbeaten in their five games to the final, picking up big wins too: 4-0 versus Mexico, 6-1 versus Spain, 7-1 versus Sweden. Vasco da Gama forward Ademir had netted eight en route to a clash with Uruguay in the final round robin game of the final group round to decide who would lift the Jules Rimet trophy.

Brazilian confidence was so high that the day before the game São Paulo's *Gazeta Esportiva* declared, 'Tomorrow we will beat Uruguay'.[101] The tie would be attended by a confirmed attendance of 173,850 spectators, but upper estimates suggest that, in fact, some 200,000 fans packed the Maracanã.[102] Despite their pedigree in pre-war tournaments, Uruguay were the clear underdogs. Goals had not been flowing as easily for them as their Brazilian counterparts and just after half-time

98 *Ibid*

99 *Birmingham Daily Gazette*, 30 June 1950

100 *Nottingham Evening Post*, 30 June 1950

101 Alex Bellos, *Futebol: The Brazilian Way of Life* (London: Bloomsbury, 2002) p.49

102 *Ibid*

on 16 July 1950 Brazil struck first through winger Albino Friaça. However, Uruguay did not lie down, outside-right Alcides Ghiggia crossing a ball on to the head of Juan Alberto Schiaffino who levelled the score at 1-1. Just 11 minutes from full time, the Maracanã was silenced a second time. Brazilian defender Bigode, arguably at fault for the equaliser, was beaten again by Ghiggia, who instead of crossing this time shot from a tight angle at close range – GOL! 2-1 the scores would remain, 2-1 to break Brazilian hearts.

The unthinkable had happened and the hosts did not know what to do. Tears and anger flowed at the final whistle, reports of suicides swept Brazil, whilst 'stadium doctors treated 169 people for fits of hysteria ... Six were taken to hospital seriously ill'.[103] The moment would become transformational for Brazil, the desperation for improvement would see a national change in style that catalysed the successes of the future. However, this moment's significance caused Ghiggia to reflect years later: 'Only three people have, with just one motion, silenced the Maracanã: Frank Sinatra, Pope John Paul II and me.'[104]

---

103 *The Guardian*, 15 March 2018

104 Alex Bellos, *Futebol: The Brazilian Way of Life* (London: Bloomsbury, 2002) p. 52

17

The 'Match of the Century' – England 3-6 Hungary (1953)

This whole book isn't an England bashing, but it just so happens that our next moment also involves them being brought back to reality again. This game is often labelled as the 'Match of the Century', so it is certainly worthy of inclusion in the 50 most important moments of all time! The Hungary side of the 1950s are a favourite for both Football History Boys, the Magical, Mighty Magyars led by their 'Galloping Major', the superb Ferenc Puskás, and their coach Gusztáv Sebes.

Hungary in the post-war years was recovering from occupations by both Germany and the USSR. It was now ruled by Mátyás Rákosi, a committed Stalinist who was fiercely loyal to the Soviet Union. This communist state lived poles apart in day-to-day life from the growing capitalist United Kingdom, but the Hungarians did not refuse to allow their footballing world to interact with the West. Gusztáv Sebes had studied other national teams closely but also benefitted from the growth in strength of domestic side Honved.

Honved were serial title winners, and being the country's national military side they were able to call up any players they so wished. This enabled some of the country's greatest talents to train together day-in, day-out, allowing the group to develop together as a single unit. As Wilson puts it, it was not just 'a handful of exceptional players', it was the fact they 'fitted together, complementing one another's abilities'.[105] The Hungarian side won the gold medal at the Olympic Games of 1952 and arrived in England on 25 November 1953 on a run of 24 unbeaten matches. However, yet again, to the English, the Magyars were less fancied because of their differing tactics to the expected norm and because England had never lost on home soil to a side outside of the British Isles.

The stage was set that November day, 105,000 fans at Wembley Stadium. The intriguing Olympic champions v the originators and self-proclaimed greats of the game. Stanley Matthews, Stan Mortenson and Alf Ramsey lined up for the hosts, whilst Ferenc Puskás, Sándor Kocsis and Zoltán Czibor started for the Magyars. England's usual WM formation was met by Hungary's inventive 2-3-3-2 formation, an adaptation that often made it play like a 4-2-4. József Bozsik, 'one of the finest playmakers in European soccer history',[106] would play alongside deeper centre-forward Nándor Hidegkuti in a creative capacity that allowed Puskás free rein and Kocsis the opportunity to grab plenty of goals. The Hungarians were well prepared for the challenge of the English on their turf, Sebes practising in the weeks preceding the fixture with the heavier English footballs, on a pitch the exact dimensions of Wembley.[107]

It took just one minute before things took a turn for the worse for Walter Winterbottom's men as Hungary took a 1-0 lead though Hidegkuti. Jackie Sewell levelled after 13 minutes but in the space of seven minutes the Magyars turned the game firmly in their favour – Nandor Hidegkuti (20) struck his second of the match whilst Puskás netted two of his own

105 Jonathan Wilson, *The Names Heard Long Ago* (New York: Bold Type Books, 2019) p.388

106 Dave Thompson, *Football FAQ* (Milwaukee: Backbeat Books, 2015) p.151

107 Jonathan Wilson, *Inverting the Pyramid: The History of Football Tactics* (London: Orion, 2010) pp.90-1

(24, 27). Mortenson managed to nab a goal just before half-time, but at the break the visitors led 4-2 – this was quite remarkable!

The second 45 minutes followed the same format as the first; Hungary dominated in every aspect of the game as they took a 6-2 lead by the 53rd minute, Hidegkuti grabbing his hat-trick with Bozsik getting in on the act too. Whilst future England boss Ramsey did score a consolation penalty it was not enough to turn the tide of the match. Hungary had torn the English apart, 35 shots versus England's five, with slick passing football that left jaws dropped.

The *Daily Mirror* the next day highlighted how Hungary were 'Masters of the ball, of position, of movement'.[108] The aftermath saw six England players never selected for the national side ever again and changes were sought because of the extent of the defeat. England were once again taught a lesson by the outside footballing world.

Billy Wright, England captain and centre-half that day, later said:

'We completely underestimated the advances that Hungary had made, and not only tactically. When we walked out at Wembley that afternoon, side by side with the visiting team, I looked down and noticed that the Hungarians had on these strange, lightweight boots, cut away like slippers under the ankle bone.

'I turned to big Stan Mortenson and said, "We should be alright here, Stan, they haven't got the proper kit."'[109]

The kit Wright referred to was football boots, something the revolutionary Hungarians also introduced to their international side. Hungary had shaken the British footballing world with the decimation of England but, despite the clear quality of the Magyars and their coaching staff, the hopes of a rematch victory in Budapest was something that would be set

---

108 *Daily Mirror*, 26 November 1953

109 Puskas, F. *Puskas on Puskas: the Life and Times of a Footballing Legend.* Edited by R. Taylor and K. Jamrich (London: Robson Books Ltd, 1998)

out for May of 1954. FA ssecretary Stanley Rous commented in the run-up to the clash: 'I assure you gentlemen the result last November was an aberration. This time England will win'.[110]

Puskás (who would go on to score 84 goals in 85 caps), Kocsis (75 in 68 games) and Hidegkuti (39 in 69) starred once more. The Hungarians secured a staggering 7-1 victory to once more humiliate the English. Harry Johnson, centre-half in November, had described the feeling of 'helplessness', 'being unable to do anything to alter the grim outlook'. With Johnson one of those dropped for the return tie, his replacement, Syd Owen, articulated the decimation handed out as 'like playing people from outer space'.[111]

The Mighty Magyars had destroyed the self-confidence of the English, who were beginning to realise that other countries had footballing lessons they could learn from. With the 1954 World Cup now on the horizon, Hungary were surely favourites to lift the trophy that summer?!

———
110 Les Scott, *End to End Stuff: The Essential Football Book* (London: Bantam Press, 2009) p.30
111 Jonathan Wilson, *Inverting the Pyramid: The History of Football Tactics*, p.90

18

The 1954 FIFA World Cup – The Miracle of Bern (1954)

The previous moment details how, in the early 1950s, the Mighty Magyars of Hungary were the most watchable, exciting and innovative side in Europe. They arrived at the 1954 World Cup in Switzerland hoping to secure a global title that would write them into the history books beyond the Olympic gold won in 1952. As ever, though, football does not always deliver as expected.

1954 was an important World Cup for a number of nations who were able to attempt qualification again after the Second World War. Japan were welcomed back but failed to make the tournament proper, whilst East Germany did not take part following the 1953 East German uprising. For West Germany, it was the start of a beautiful international footballing journey.

They would line up in the 16-team format, organised uniquely for a World Cup into groups of four, featuring two seeded and two unseeded countries. There would only be two group fixtures per team, however, with each seeded team playing unseeded ones and avoiding each other. The final oddity saw the quarter-finals drawn with the four group winners taking one side of the draw, with the four group runners-up making up the other half.

Hungary hadn't lost a match since May 1950 and the Mighty Magyars waltzed through their group with a 9-0 opening win against South Korea with a Sándor Kocsis hat-trick and a Ferenc Puskás brace. They followed this up with a magnificent thrashing of West Germany 8-3, Kocsis this time netting four whilst Nándor Hidegkuti opened his World Cup account with two. With Hungary safely through, West Germany would need a play-off victory against Turkey to secure their place in the quarter-finals, a Max Morlock hat-trick doing the job in the 7-2 thumping.

Elsewhere, losses to Austria and the reigning champions Uruguay would send the Scottish home from their first World Cup, conceding eight and failing to score. England, meanwhile, drew 4-4 versus Belgium before beating hosts Switzerland 2-0 to secure their passage to the quarter-finals, a mighty improvement on four years previous! In the fourth group, a big win over Mexico, followed by a draw with Yugoslavia, would see the Brazilians top the rankings in their pursuit of a first Jules Rimet trophy.

Devastatingly for the Hungarians, talisman Puskás picked up a hairline ankle fracture in the victory against West Germany. This ruled him out of a clash with Brazil that would be later labelled the 'Battle of Bern', due to its brutality. Yorkshireman Arthur Ellis refereed the tie that saw three players dismissed, including Hungary's József Bozsik and Brazil's Nílton Santos for a punch-up, and Brazilian forward Humberto late on for kicking out at Magyar Gyula Lorant. Ellis later remarked, 'I thought it was going to be the greatest game I'd ever seen … but they behaved like animals. It was a disgrace.'[112] Even off the pitch the violence continued, and Puskás (spectating on the sidelines) was reported to have hit Brazilian defender Pinheiro in the face with a bottle, although he escaped unpunished.[113]

---

112 *The Independent*, 9 June 1998
113 Alex Bellos, *Futebol: The Brazilian Way of Life*, p.100

The West Germans beat the Yugoslavs 2-0 in their last-eight tie, setting up a draw with Austria in the semi-finals. Morlock was again the hero for the Germans as they put Austria to the sword 6-1 and earned a well-deserved final place. Hungary, still missing Puskás, faced off against the well-fancied Uruguay side who had sent England home 4-2. The semi-final was another ding-dong battle, Hungary going from 2-0 up to drawing 2-2 after 90 minutes due to two late Uruguay strikes. Into extra time they went ... step up Kocsis again! The future Barcelona star netted twice in five minutes in additional time to send the Magyars into the final that could make or break them as a 'Golden Generation'. The defeat for Uruguay was the first ever for them at World Cups, winning the previous two they had participated in (1930 and 1950).

That brings us to 4 July 1954: West Germany v Hungary for the final of the World Cup in Wankdorf Stadium, Bern. Over 62,000 fans packed the stands in torrential rain to watch the 'miracle' match unfold. 'The World's greatest team, against the World's enemy. East vs. West. Capitalism vs. Communism.'[114] An unfit Puskás was included in the final line-up and justified his selection with the opening goal after just six minutes. Zoltán Czibor added a second two minutes later and the Germans looked in trouble at 0-2 down – all was going to plan. However, the final was not yet lost; the West Germans surprisingly struck back to make it 2-2 at the break through Morlock and Helmut Rahn. Everything was to play for in the last 45 minutes of the World Cup.

The Hungarians dominated the second half but stunningly, in the 84th minute, Helmut Rahn – the West German outside-right – scored with an individual piece of magic and nicked the tie to shock the watching world. The final whistle couldn't come soon enough for the Germans, with Puskás having a late equaliser correctly ruled out for offside; but when it did

---

114 Ben Jones, '1954 World Cup: The Miracle of Bern', *The Football History Boys* (15 February 2013) https://www.thefootballhistoryboys.com/2013/02/1954-world-cup-miracle-of-bern.html

sound it was official ... newbies West Germany had beaten the Magnificent Magyars. The Miracle of Bern had taken place!

For Hungary it is still considered the 'greatest disappointment Hungarian sport has known', the national team never reaching these great heights again to this day. Whilst for West Germany the significance was clear, Franz Beckenbauer remembering later: 'For anybody who grew up in the misery of the post-war years, Bern was an extraordinary inspiration. The entire country regained its self esteem.'[115] The miracle is without doubt one of Germany's greatest sporting moments, certainly in World Cup history. A new international superpower had been born, whilst another – Hungary – had been snuffed out.

---

115 Jonathan Wilson, *The Names Heard Long Ago* (New York: Bold Type Books, 2019)

19

The Birth of the European Cup – *Los Blancos* Make it Five in a Row (1955–60)

The 1950s had been a decade of change, both within football but also in Europe politically, with nations working out their positions on the world stage following the war. Britain was a shifting place too, the country was 'relatively speaking, on the sidelines … losing an empire and searching for a role'.[116] Developments in social policy, such as the growing welfare state, and a growth in the desire for entertainment in the post-war years, had seen life change for the ordinary Briton. This entertainment, for many, would be satisfied by a love of sport and the European Cup played its part within that.

The idea of continental football was not something totally new to the 1950s. Whilst British football had grown through the Victorian era, other European countries were quick to found football associations and codify their games. These countries began to toy with the idea of playing each other on the continental stage, one particular trailblazer being the Challenge Cup, played between countries in the Austro-Hungarian Empire. Founded in 1897, it mainly featured

---

116 Richard Holt, *Sport and the British* (Oxford: Oxford University, 1989) p.278

teams from Vienna (Austria), Budapest (Hungary) and Prague (Czechoslovakia). The knockout tournament lasted until 1911 and was won three times by Weiner Athletiksport Club of Austria. Its success led to other competitions such as the Austrian Cup (1919) and the Mitropa Cup (1927).[117]

The Mitropa Cup allowed central European football clubs to develop their game in the inter-war years. As the reputation grew, other nations joined this growing tournament, the English FA sending some officials over to Czechoslovakia and Hungary to referee the two-leg final in 1935.[118] This competition ran until 1992, Hungary producing 16 winners, Vasas (Hungary) the most successful club with six titles. This cup competition could certainly be seen as a forerunner of the European Cup, laying the foundations for continental collaboration on a grander scale.

The European Cup stormed on to the scene in 1955. The competition was initially the brainchild of French sports newspaper *L'Equipe*. Jacques Goddet – the paper's owner, as well as editor Gabriel Hanot, Jacques de Ryswick and Jacques Ferran – of the paper's football section, petitioned the newly founded UEFA (June 1954) to organise a continent-wide, annual tournament. Part of their inspiration was also taken from the Campeonato Sudamericano de Campeones, which had started in 1948, bringing together champions from across South America. Ferran also cites that the claim of the British media that Wolverhampton Wanderers were 'world champions' because they had beaten Honved and Spartak Moscow in 1953/54 inspired Hanot to create a tournament for teams to prove it.[119]

117 Gareth Thomas, 'The Birth of the European Cup: L'Equipe, Los Blancos and the Glorious 1950s', *The Football History Boys* (17 November 2016) https://www.thefootballhistoryboys.com/2016/11/the-birth-of-european-cup-lequipe-los.html

118 *Lancashire Evening Post*, 27 August 1935

119 UEFA website, '50 Years of the European Cup', *UEFA* (October 2004) https://www.uefa.com/newsfiles/240459.pdf

'Before we declare that Wolverhampton Wanderers are invincible, let them go to Moscow and Budapest. And then there are other internationally renowned clubs: Milan and Real Madrid to name but two. A club world championship, or at least a European one – larger, more meaningful and more prestigious than the Mitropa Cup ... should be launched.' Gabriel Hanot.[120]

In September 1955, with *L'Equipe*'s idea taken on board, 16 teams were entered for the first-ever European Cup. Sides included Milan (Italy), Aarhus (Denmark), Anderlecht (Belgium), Partizan (Yugoslavia), PSV Eindhoven (Netherlands), Rapid Wien (Austria), Real Madrid (Spain), Sporting CP (Portugal) and Stade de Reims (France). Scotland, meanwhile, sent Hibernian to participate but the English league champions Chelsea were told to withdraw from entering by the Football League. The Blues agreed to the request, jointly admitting with the administrators that the 'league programme does not allow for "six or eight" visitors from abroad'.[121]

That very first version of the European Cup was set up as a straight, two-leg knockout tournament. Real Madrid progressed 7-0 on aggregate over Swiss side Servette in the first round and then beat Partizan 4-3, whilst Milan beat Saarbrücken (Saarland) 7-5 and Rapid Wein 8-3. That set up a mouth-watering tie as the champions of Spain took on the champions of Italy in the semi-finals. The first leg, at the Santiago Bernabéu, was won 4-2 by Real Madrid, and despite losing 2-1 in Italy Real were into the first-ever European Cup Final.

Stade Reims were the opponent in Paris in June 1956, having beaten Scottish side Hibs 3-0 in the semis. UEFA report that Reims made a blistering start, Michel Leblond

---

120 Edward Couzens-Lake, *Mapping the Pitch: Football Coaches, Players and Formations Through The Ages* (Maidenhead: Meyer & Meyer Sport Ltd., 2015) p.161

121 *West London Observer*, 29 July 1955

netting after six minutes before Jean Templin made it 2-0 just four minutes later. Leaving Los Blancos with an uphill task, Alfredo Di Stéfano brought the Spaniards back into the match after 14 minutes, before Héctor Rial levelled the scores at half-time. Reims took the lead again in the second half, but Real Madrid once again equalised quickly to leave things tied heading into the last 15 minutes of the pulsating final. It would be Rial who popped up in the 79th minute to secure the victory for Madrid – 'losing his marker with a deft first touch, he was free to stab the winner inside the far post'.[122] We had our first champions of Europe!

In the following season, Manchester United would ignore the continued call of the English authorities to reject the advances of the European Cup, joining the fray as the first English representatives. They saw off Anderlecht 10-0 on aggregate before beating Borussia Dortmund over two legs, added to by an impressive 6-5 aggregate victory against Spaniards Athletic Bilbao. Defending champions Real Madrid were the next opponents, a 3-1 loss in Spain leaving a mighty task at Old Trafford if United were to reach the final that would be hosted by the Santiago Bernabéu. Rial and Raymond Kopa scored for the visitors in a 2-2 draw and gave Real Madrid the opportunity to defend their title on home turf. *Los Blancos* did so, Di Stéfano and Francisco Gento banking a 2-0 win over Italian side Fiorentina in front of a reported 120,000 fans.[123] Madrid had two in a row!

This would be made a hat-trick of trophies by Real in 1957/58 with the third edition of the European Cup featuring its first entrants from Northern Ireland (Glenavon) and Ireland (Shamrock Rovers). Heysel Stadium, Belgium, was the venue that would host the final this campaign and once more the Spaniards would dominate. Di Stéfano netted nine goals en

---

122 UEFA website, 'Madrid bounce back to start era of dominance', *UEFA* (1 September 2014) https://www.uefa.com/uefachampionsleague/news/newsid=2155985.html?iv=true

123 *Birmingham Daily Post*, 31 May 1957

route to the final as Hungarian side Vasas were put away 4-2 on aggregate in the semi-finals. Manchester United again made the last four, but their squad, decimated by the Munich Air Disaster (Moment 20), lost 4-0 in the second leg at the San Siro in Milan to allow the Italians the right to take on Madrid. AC Milan were left as runners-up, losing 3-2 after extra time: Di Stéfano, Rial and Gento on the scoresheet in Belgium.[124]

Year on year, the tournament was expanded, and 28 teams qualified for the fourth edition of European competition. Wolves, who were part of the inspiration for the European Cup, made their first appearance. However, it was not an easy debut, a 2-2 draw at Molineux followed by a 2-1 loss to Germans Schalke in the return leg and Wolves were out. Real Madrid, meanwhile, stormed through the rounds yet again and once more Stade Reims would be their final opponents at the Neckarstadion, Stuttgart. Enrique Mateos opened the scoring for *Los Blancos* before that man Di Stéfano added a second. Just like in 1955/56, the French side were beaten and Di Stefano had scored in each of the four finals they had won. Newspapers labelled them 'Fantastic!'[125] – Would the Real dominance ever end?

That brings us to 1959/60 – Real Madrid attempting a fifth consecutive European Cup success. Hungarian Ferenc Puskás (now 33) had joined *Los Blancos* in 1958, making them an even greater threat than before and the target was a place at Hampden Park, Glasgow, for the 1960 final. This season saw a mouth-watering *El Clásico* clash in the semi-finals, Real Madrid versus Catalonia's Barcelona. The experience of Real showed, the defending champions putting their rivals to the sword in a 6-2 aggregate demolition. Puskás netted three of the six whilst Di Stefano scored twice, leaving German team Eintracht Frankfurt waiting in Scotland in May 1960. With

124 *Coventry Evening Telegraph*, 29 May 1958

125 *Daily Herald*, 4 June 1958

almost 130,000 spectators watching perhaps the best side of all time, *Los Blancos* did not disappoint. It was a night described as 'the greatest show on earth', Di Stefano seizing a hat-trick, while Puskás scored a remarkable four in the 7-3 thrashing.[126] Real Madrid had made it five in a row, their stars showed their quality and the European Cup was well and truly theirs!

The European Cup, or, as we now know it, the Champions League, is perhaps the most glorious tournament a professional footballer can win at club level. Europe's premier cup competition is worth millions and millions of pounds in advertising, television revenue and prize money to those who qualify. We must reflect on those important infancy years, though, as a cup that gripped a continent.

---

126 *Aberdeen Evening Express*, 19 May 1960

20

Munich Air Disaster (1958)

Moment 20 is an incredibly sad one; however, it is vitally important nonetheless. The majority of football fans will already know about the Munich Air Disaster of 1958, its impact not just touching British shores but on continental Europe too. On 6 February 1958, Manchester United Football Club were changed forever with what happened at Munich–Riem Airport in West Germany following a European Cup tie.

The plane that crashed attempting to take off in the snow that fateful day contained the famous Busby Babes. A side managed by the legendary Sir Matthew Busby, recruited from the local area by scout Joe Armstrong and coached from a young age by Busby's assistant Jimmy Murphy. The Babes, with an average age of just 21 years old, won the First Division title in 1955/56, 11 points clear of second-placed Blackpool. They followed up the feat the very next year with a defence of their league title and the hopes of success in the European Cup to come. These boys had the world at their feet, ready to take on a continental challenge and prove the hype that surrounded them as correct.

On that winter's day of 1954, United had just beaten Red Star Belgrade of Yugoslavia in advance of the semi-finals of the European competition. Their British Airways plane had stopped in Munich to refuel and, with snow falling, two take-off attempts had already been abandoned. The pilot that day

decided on another attempt in favour of an overnight stop
– how costly that decision became. Skidding on the slush of
the runway, flight 609 ploughed into a fence, then a house,
at speed.[127]

The initial reactions in British newspapers the following
day were predictably emotional, the *Birmingham Daily
Post* noting that some of the injuries to survivors whilst
'comparatively unimportant to an ordinary civilian may, to a
footballer, mean the end of a playing career'. They continued,
'a club whose performances in post-war football have captured
the imagination of the sporting public ... will have to be
virtually rebuilt'.[128] The *Daily Mirror* meanwhile wondered
how 'the most successful of post-war English teams' could
rebuild itself 'from the shattering tragedy of the Munich air
crash'.[129]

Heartbreakingly, the reaction of the newspapers was
accurate as 23 of 38 passengers were killed in Germany. The
Busby Babes were ripped apart as Geoff Bent (25), Roger
Byrne (28), Eddie Colman (21), Duncan Edwards (21), Mark
Jones (24), David Pegg (22), Tommy Taylor (26) and Billy
Whelan (22) all succumbed to their injuries. Additionally,
Jackie Blanchflower (24) and Johnny Berry (31) would never
play football again. It wasn't just footballers killed, either:
three club staff, eight journalists and two other passengers
lost their lives as a result of Munich. For Manchester United
it was the destruction of perhaps their best-ever side and for
the families of those killed and fans alike, it is a night that will
never, ever be forgotten.

In the aftermath, United chairman Harold Hardman
was stubborn in his insistence that the club would finish the
season. He declared: 'We carry on. Even if it means being
heavily defeated we shall fulfil the season's programme. We

---

127 *Daily Express*, 6 February 2008
128 *Birmingham Daily Post*, 7 February 1958
129 *Daily Mirror*, 8 February 1958

have a duty to the public and a duty to football to carry out.'[130] Manager Matt Busby, who survived the accident, also vowed to rebuild the club and stayed on as boss until 1969 with the intention of making Manchester United great once more.

United played their first game post-Munich staggeringly just 13 days later, facing Sheffield Wednesday in the fifth round of the FA Cup. Assistant manager Jimmy Murphy, who was also manager of the Welsh national team, was not with the team in Munich and he took the reins on 19 February 1958. Of those involved in the crash, only Harry Gregg and Bill Foulkes were fit to play a part and so the rest of the matchday squad was made up of youth or reserve players. A stunning performance, however, saw United win the tie 3-0, 20-year-old debutant Shay Brennan netting twice with 16-year-old Alex Dawson firing in the other strike. It was an emotional night at Old Trafford, with fans and players wearing black armbands and observing a two-minute silence in memory of those lost at Munich.[131]

To complete their season, United made a number of signings to bolster their squad. Ernie Taylor (Blackpool) and Stan Crowther (Aston Villa) joined, whilst numerous players also joined from non-league team Bishop Auckland.[132] The disaster became an opportunity for many players in the reserve and youth sides at Old Trafford; along with Brennan and Dawson, other places in the squad were filled by those who filled the gaps of the sadly deceased players. United would finish the season a respectable ninth in the First Division. A remarkable FA Cup, meanwhile, would lead them to the final, where they finished runners-up to Bolton Wanderers.

The recovery process was led by Matt Busby and his staff, first lifting the FA Cup in 1963 versus Leicester City. This was followed by the First Division title in 1965 and 1967, a

---

130 *Ibid*

131 *Birmingham Evening Post*, 20 February 1958

132 Stephen Morrin, *The Munich Air Disaster* (Ireland: Gill & Macmillan, 2007) pp.147-50

significant achievement for the revamped side. The climax of this process was reached ten years later, in May 1968, at Wembley Stadium. Busby's United marched to the European Cup Final, the journey that had begun a decade previously on that night in Munich. Crash survivors Bobby Charlton and Bill Foulkes lined up against Portuguese side Benfica in front of over 90,000 spectators.

United lifted the trophy 4-1 after extra time to become champions of Europe for the first time in their history. Bobby Charlton scored twice in the victory and newspapers were understandably delighted, remarking how this 1968 side had invoked the spirit of the 1958 Busby Babes. *The Times* reported: 'Foulkes and Charlton typify the loyalty that inspired this great Manchester club ... last night at Wembley I am certain each of them played as devotedly for that lost past as for the living present.'[133] As Mellor notes, the final became an almost 'quasi-religious experience',[134] as Manchester United finally fulfilled the promises made by chairman Harold Hardman and Matt Busby to rebuild the club in the days that followed Munich. There is no doubt that Munich is worthy of its inclusion in this list.

---

133 Gavin Mellor in Paul Darby, Martin Johnes and Gavin Mellor (eds), *Soccer and Disaster* (London: Routledge, 2005) p.153

134 *Ibid*

1961–70

21

The Football League Removes
the Maximum Wage (1961)

If there is one thing football can't escape in the modern age, it is money. It is everywhere. From Tottenham's new £1bn stadium, to the cost of a pie on the terraces of your local side – it is always a topic of debate. So far, in the 50 moments we have seen, the effect commercialism has had on the game is clear – starting with the Victorian professionals and leading to the first television broadcast in 1937. Today, footballers' wages are often discussed, and for good reason. The sheer amount of money the average Premier League player receives today is astounding.

But has this always been the case? The simple answer is no. Following the end of the Second World War, employment was high and the public had money to spend, but little to spend it on. This was born mainly out of rationing. Still in effect in the immediate years after the war, the luxuries of modern life were under heavy restrictions as the country attempted to reconstruct itself from the conflict. Attending football matches, therefore, became part of a 'broader outburst of pleasure-seeking'.[135] Footballers were not so impressed,

---

135 James Walvin, *The People's Game: A History of Football Revisited* (Mainstream, 1994)

however. Despite spectatorism at an all-time high, footballers' wages had barely increased and in 1946 were at only £8-a-week. Alongside an early retirement age, these salaries were just not good enough. The debate didn't subside in the following decade as the law on maximum wage capped their pay at £20-a-week and no higher.

In stepped Jimmy Hill. The average football fan may remember him best for his presenting of *Match of the Day*, but his influence on the modern game is far greater. In 1961 Hill was the chairman of the PFA. Under his leadership, the union campaigned hard for the removal of the maximum wage and even threatened a strike in the process. Perhaps surprisingly, given modern views, the general public became increasingly sympathetic and receptive to the players.[136] Furthermore, those playing were certain with where they stood. The *Birmingham Daily Post* was quick to record the feelings of a Derby County player in December 1960.

'We have had a meeting and gone into the matter carefully. As players with a second division club, we are fighting for greater freedom over contracts and an increase in the minimum wage.'[137]

The Football League was at a crossroads. In the years leading up to 1961, an increasing number of British players began to find success abroad. Most noticeable was Welsh centre-back John Charles after his transfer to Juventus in 1956. As well as earning more money in Italy, Charles's overall life saw multiple benefits, like a villa on the coast and greater bonuses. Furthermore, he employed an agent to engineer the move.[138] Such transfers would become increasingly common as the 1950s came to an end. By the start of the 1960s, something needed to change.

---

136 Matthew Taylor, *The Association Game*

137 *Birmingham Daily Post*, 8 December 1960

138 Richard Holt and Tony Mason, *Sport in Britain: 1945-2000* (Oxford: Blackwell, 2000) p.80

Illegal payments to players began to become prevalent in the game. This practice was seen clearest in Sunderland following a scandal which saw fines and bans for leading players and officials.[139] Such moments caused a rift between the PFA and the Football League, leading to an increasing demand to remove the maximum wage. The conversations between the two associations were bitter and employers were generally reluctant to relent. However, the threat of a strike was too great for the Football League, eventually changing their mind and removing the maximum wage in January 1961.

Why is this important? Just look at the modern game. In the 1960s, the PFA's arguments had credit and class. It was a movement which was justifiably backed by the public and genuinely campaigned for principles and fair play. Today, it is common to read news articles about players not happy to be on 'only £300,000-a-week' – perhaps by understanding Hill's campaign better it will help us all see what the game could and should be about. The union that Billy Meredith had fought to create 50 years earlier had found its place in the game and players had a voice which was listened to. Its influence would only continue to grow and to this day continues to be one of football's most important institutions.

---

139 *Ibid*, p.81

22

England Win the
World Cup (1966)

The 1950s had been a turbulent time for the English national team. Defeat to the US in the 1950 World Cup and humiliation at the hands of Hungary three years later meant a rapid overhaul was needed to the 'English' game. What was to come was proof that long-term planning and patience was key to success. Of course, in football history this notion is nothing new – take Brazil's defeat to Uruguay in 1950. The 'maracanazo' (Moment 16) was used as a catalyst for a change in style, leading to their future successes. Humiliation for the South Americans meant even the smallest of details, like the colour of kit, needed to be rethought and reimagined.[140] England would need a similar overhaul.

Britain in 1966 was in the midst of mass social change. Two years prior to this The Beatles had taken the world by storm, forcing an evolution to both fashion and social attitudes. Britain was losing its image of posh toffs and bowler hats and was now the trendiest nation on Earth. In football, England had undergone a similar transformation. Firstly, a full-time, first-team coach was employed. Alf Ramsey would take over

---

140 Alex Bellos, *Futebol: The Brazilian Way of Life* (London: Bloomsbury, 2002) pp.43-66

the reins and amazingly become the first manager in English football history to pick the starting XI. Previously a group of selectors had chosen who would compete for the Three Lions.

Most importantly was formation development. Finally the tried and tested WM style was gone in favour of a more progressive 4-3-3.

'Their technical brilliance and new tactics completely kyboshed our old WM formation in just 90 minutes.'[141]

Bobby Robson's words were true, and according to his fellow Geordie Bobby Charlton it would be Alf Ramsey who paid the highest price for the defeat at Wembley in 1953. Losing his place in the side, the painful embarrassment at the hands of magical Magyars would later help him to secure the national job with a determination to do it his way.[142]

Ramsey had tremendous faith in his side and believed they would win the World Cup.[143] England were considered amongst the pre-tournament favourites. Indeed, Brazil (winners in 1958 and 1962), Italy and West Germany all seemingly offered superior sides, but with home advantage the founders of the game may just have enough.

Despite this, Britain was well and truly in a state of 'World Cup fever'. The excitement and press coverage was so intense that it led to an article in the *Walsall Observer* asking, 'Are you weary of hearing nothing else but World Cup ... World Cup ... World Cup? World Cup Widows unite!'[144] Elsewhere, the *Coventry Evening Telegraph* made it clear to those looking to escape the 'World Cup epidemic', that BBC Two would be a safe haven.[145] It would be the extensive television coverage on BBC One and ITV which helped to distinguish this World Cup from previous editions. It gave the competition a modern

---

141 Bobby Robson in Bobby Charlton, *1966: My World Cup Story* (London: Yellow Jersey, 2016) p.37

142 Bobby Charlton, *1966: My World Cup Story*, p.38

143 *Birmingham Daily Post*, 11 July 1966

144 *Walsall Observer*, 6 July 1966

145 *Coventry Evening Telegraph*, 11 July 1966

feel, in keeping with the modernisation of wider society, and meant the tournament was well and truly a national experience.[146]

England defied the odds to reach the final where a youthful West German side would await. The match at Wembley is perhaps one of the most documented and reminisced events in modern British history. Despite feverish scenes amongst English fans, most neutrals wanted West Germany to win, citing 'boring' football as the prime reason.[147] Following a last-minute West German equaliser, the final score was locked at 2-2. As extra time progressed, the Germans looked increasingly fatigued, and, buoyed on by the home support, Geoff Hurst scored two more goals to add to his one in the first half. By doing this, he became the first and only player to score a hat-trick in a World Cup Final. On the other hand, controversy was not far away, as a suspect Russian linesman awarded Hurst's second when the ball looked to have bounced on the goal-line … was it in? It's up to you!

This moment may get a few Welsh, Scottish and Irish fans groaning, but it had a far greater impact than we can imagine. In fact, in Wales some newspapers ran editorials the day after the final rejoicing in the victory and claiming it as a 'British' one.[148] In Scotland, although there was far less revelling in victory, newspapers like the *Aberdeen Evening News* still ran with the headline 'England Champions of the World'.[149] There was also an abundance of British flags as opposed to St George's crosses at Wembley during the tournament. The 1960s had begun to help the United Kingdom to find a new identity and the 1966 World Cup victory for England

---

146 Tony Mason, 'England 1966: Traditional or Modern', *National Identity and Global Sports Events: Culture, Politics and Spectacle in the Olympics and the Football World Cup* (New York: SUNY, 2006)

147 Roger Hutchinson, *'66: The Inside Story of England's 1966 World Cup Triumph* (London: Random House, 2011)

148 Tony Mason, E*ngland 1966: Traditional or Modern?*

149 *Aberdeen Evening News*, 30 July 1966

was central to it. In victory, England had truly reflected an evolving Britain behind it. Gone was the rustic, antiquated style of the past. The nation had truly shown its openness to change and new ideas. Looking at the state of the country today, perhaps this is a lesson which needs repeating.

23

The Lisbon Lions (1967)

By 1967 the European Cup was still in its infancy. Despite being just over a decade old, it went from strength to strength, building its reputation as the finest club competition on Earth. What made the European Cup so successful was its scope. Earlier international club competitions had been played in the shape of the Mitropa Cup (1927) and the Latin Cup (1949), but these were limited to central and western Europe. In the 1953/54 season, English champions Wolverhampton Wanderers had used their status to host Europe's best clubs at Molineux. The exhibitions were dubbed 'floodlit friendlies' due to their late kick-off times. Frequently running out as victors, it was not long before the British press had dubbed them 'Champions of the World'. The European Cup devised by *L'Equipe* magazine in France set out to determine once and for all who the best side in Europe was.

Tactically speaking, the winners of the tournament since 1956 had favoured rigid, tactical styles. Inter Milan had dominated the competition in the mid-1960s, adopting a platform of *catenaccio*. This would see four man-marking defenders, with a sweeper to pick up any loose balls. Furthermore, with fast and effective counter-attacks, the Italians would have chances to score. Paranoid, negative and brutal, the style would be reviled in Britain, particularly after

Liverpool's semi-final defeat to the Milan side in 1965.[150] Similar to modern-day 'park-the-bus' or aeroplane, as José Mourinho would tell you, the tactics were branded as anti-football.

It was no surprise that Inter made it to the final in 1967. Meeting them in Lisbon were Scottish champions Celtic who, although only beating weaker opposition, had impressed the footballing community with their attacking flair – scoring 16 goals in their eight games. Jock Stein's side had also won the domestic league and both national cups. The European Cup, therefore, would be the final piece of an unprecedented quadruple.

Pre-match conversation was dominated by tactics. The *Reading Evening Post* featured the headline, 'It's an all-out attack plan for Celtic heroes'. The article continues to note that the game would be a 'battle of tactics'. Inter, it was reported, were likely to try to slow the game down and gain an ascendancy in midfield before launching quick and explosive counter-attacks.[151] The general atmosphere before the game was one of battles. Celtic, it seemed, were representing the future of football. Stein, aware of the animosity towards the Italians and their style of play, was quick to quell any ill-feeling.

'We will play an attacking game. We've come to play a game of football, not to fight a war.' Jock Stein[152]

The final got off to the worst possible start for the Bhoys – a goal down within seven minutes following a penalty from Sandro Mazzola (son of Valentino). In theory, this would suit the Italians perfectly. With a narrow lead to defend, surely *catenaccio* would prevail once more. As the second half progressed, however, the positive attacking style of Celtic began to pay off as first Thomas Gemmell

---

150 Jonathan Wilson, *Inverting the Pyramid: The History of Football Tactics* (UK: Orion, 2010) p.188

151 *Reading Evening Post*, 25 May 1967

152 *Ibid*

equalised before an 84th-minute finish from Stevie Chalmers won the match. In reality, the second-half had been a brutal onslaught of attacking football which Inter couldn't contain.[153] *Catenaccio* had been exposed and would take years to recover. Stein was quick to praise the attacking mentality of his side: 'This was a triumph for attacking football against defensive methods.'

Even the opposition were able to see the beauty of Celtic's play. The team was nicknamed the Lisbon Lions after the game, as they became the first British side to win the ultimate prize in club football. Furthermore, the whole side was born within 30 miles of Parkhead – Celtic's home ground. This, coupled with an upbringing of 'impoverishment, illness and intolerance', had meant the side represented far more than the badge they wore on their green and white hoops.[154] Celtic's match winner Stevie Chalmers had even survived tuberculosis meningitis in 1955 in order to help create one of football's finest stories.

On the pitch, victory in Lisbon would open football up to new tactical invention, as Matt Busby's Manchester United would emerge victorious the following season before the mighty Ajax and Bayern teams ruled the continent for half a decade. Football was changing once more and Celtic were to thank. In Italy, Inter would take the next 30 years to fully recover to the heights of the 1960s. In 1972 Cruyff's Ajax had further compounded *catenaccio's* decline with a new tactical innovation – 'total football'.[155] Ironically, it was with José Mourinho's rebranded *catenaccio* that the *Nerazzurri* swept aside all that was before them and won a historic treble in 2010.

The importance of the Lisbon Lions grows stronger with every newspaper, documentary and memoir. It remains perhaps

---

153 Jonathan Wilson, *Inverting the Pyramid*, p.192

154 Glasgow 1967: The Lisbon Lions, BBC Documentary (2017)

155 John Foot, *Calcio: A History of Italian Football*, p.229

the greatest example of football being about a community and an identity above all else. The green half of Glasgow kicked, headed and tackled every ball that their heroes did. The Lisbon Lions were a family whose legacy will be fondly remembered for decades to come.

24

The Football War (1969)

Just over 100 years into its codification, football had become the world's game. We have already seen how the game was disseminated through Britain, Europe and South America, but what is truly incredible about the game is its ability to become integral to communities in each and every area of the globe. By 1969 the World Cup had of course played host to the major players in football, but also unfancied nations like Egypt, the Dutch East Indies (now Indonesia) and North Korea. It had brought these countries into the wider public eye, often for the first time, and the benefits of such publicity offered an incentive some nations wouldn't let go of easily. The 1970 World Cup was to offer two places for North American nations.

If the World Cup had brought nations together, the Second World War did quite the opposite. After Allied victory, two ideologies split the globe – capitalism (backed by the US) and communism (backed by the USSR). In Honduras the 'red scare' of communism had seen a shift in power following a right-wing military coup by General Oswaldo Lopez Arellano. Despite backing from big US business, economic immaturity led to a country on the brink. The general needed someone to blame – and who was it? Salvadoran immigrants.

The 20th century had seen vast swathes of the El Salvador population cross the border into neighbouring Honduras due to over-population and a lack of working opportunities.[156] Tensions between the two nations began to heighten. So what better to defuse the aggravation than a football match? In 1969 the two sides had won their respective World Cup qualifying groups and would be drawn together in a play-off. The winner would earn the right to play in bordering Mexico a year later. Two initial fixtures were arranged and tensions couldn't have been higher. This was to be the most important 180 minutes in either nation's football history.[157]

The first leg, played in Honduras, was won by the home nation 1-0. Prior to the game, the Salvadoran side had complained about the behaviour of the Honduras fans. Intent on disrupting the sleep of the away team's players, the Hondurans had partied long into the night outside the El Salvador hotel. Following the match, violence had broken out between opposing sets of supporters. Economic, political and cultural tensions had well and truly spilled over on to the football pitch.

A week later, the sides met again, this time in San Salvador. The victimisation of El Salvadoran immigrants had been used to fire up both players and fans before the match, leading to an incredibly hostile atmosphere. During the national anthems, the Honduran flag was replaced with a dirty rag, further antagonising the supporters within the ground. Unsurprisingly, El Salvador won the match 3-0. Despite a clear 3-1 aggregate victory, 1969 FIFA rules meant the fixture was tied at one win a piece, leading to yet another match, this time in neutral Mexico.[158]

Following a 2-2 draw, El Salvador emerged as winners after extra time. After the final whistle, violence began to break out, at first in the stands of the Azteca and later in

---

156 Jim Murphy, *The 10 Football Matches That Changed the World: And The One That Didn't* (London: Biteback, 2014)

157 *Ibid*

158 Jim Murphy, *The 10 Football Matches That Changed the World: And The One That Didn't*

Honduras. Infuriated locals took out their anger on the El Salvadoran immigrants by burning down their homes and forcing them to return to their nation of origin. The match had even made the news in Britain as the *Reading Evening Post* ran the story under the headline, 'Only a Game'.[159] For Honduras and El Salvador, this was more than a game. The football pitch in Mexico City had been, for those playing and those in the respective nations, a battlefield. It was reported that at the final whistle the Honduran players 'threw themselves on the muddy field and wept like children'.[160]

With their natives under threat, El Salvador cut off ties between the nations and two weeks later declared war. Despite only lasting 100 hours the conflict saw more than 6,000 dead and tensions, would struggle to recover – even to this day. Future matches between the two countries have been relatively common in World Cup qualifying and Gold Cup fixtures. Honduras have fared the better of the two in recent years and even qualified for both the 2010 and 2014 World Cups.

In reality, football of course wasn't the reason for the war as its reasons ran far deeper than a 90-minute match. However, what it does show is the sheer power football can have on a population. It highlights the national pride and identity that come with the sport. Losing to El Salvador meant the Hondurans wouldn't be represented on the world stage, with their identity and national pride taking a severe battering. This may well have been the straw that broke the camel's back. Football is clearly intertwined with the nation and since 1969 they have eventually reached the World Cup twice. Today, we are able to see the good the game can bring as their national side is a cornerstone for principles in an otherwise fractious country.

---

159 *Reading Evening Post*, 28 June 1969
160 *Liverpool Echo*, 28 June 1969

25

Italy vs West Germany – The Game of the Century (1970)

One of the greatest elements of football is its ability to create some amazing rivalries. One of these is between the international sides of Italy and Germany. In 1970 Germany was split into the east and the west. It was the west that became the more successful on the football pitch. Having reached the World Cup Final in 1966, and after defeating reigning champions England in the quarter-finals, they were favourites to win their semi-final against fellow Europeans Italy at the Azteca Stadium, Mexico City.

The relationship between the two nations had been frosty since the Second World War, where both nations' fascist governments had fallen amidst massive conflict and loss. In terms of football, the Germans had gone from strength to strength following the 'Miracle of Bern' (Moment 18), with the Italians taking years to recover from the Superga Air Disaster (Moment 15) in 1949. Italy did, however, win the European Championships in 1968. Captained by Giacinto Facchetti, the *Azzurri* had dug deep to overcome a tricky Yugoslavia in Rome. The victory had helped the nation to forget the defeat to North Korea in 1966 and bring the country together following student protests, which had questioned traditional Italian values earlier in 1968.

West Germany hadn't qualified for the Euros in 1968, despite entering the mini-group stage as top seeds. Finalists at the 1966 World Cup though, they would be regarded as one of the teams to beat in Mexico. They took their magnificent form into the World Cup, scoring an impressive ten goals in the group stage as Morocco, Bulgaria and Peru were all comfortably dispatched. The spearhead of the attack, Gerd Müller, had scored six and was in incredible form.

In stark contrast, Italy had managed to win their group despite only scoring one goal. A narrow victory over Sweden was followed by disappointing draws to Uruguay and Israel. The matches were described by Pelé as 'sterile' as *catenaccio* was deployed once more.[161] The tactical system, so comprehensively picked apart in 1967, appeared to be a winning formula in international football.

In the next round, the shackles of *catenaccio* were removed as Italy comfortably beat hosts Mexico before West Germany beat the aforementioned England 3-2 after extra time. The *Azzurri* had been seen as a different team to that of the group stage. Indeed, the 'sparkling champagne' football, spearheaded by the mercurial Luigi Riva, had helped them to regain confidence going into the semi-final.[162] The stage, therefore, would be set for an epic showdown in front of a 107,000-capacity crowd in the Mexican capital. An even greater incentive was that meeting the victors in the final would be the great Brazilian side of Pelé, Jairzinho and Carlos Alberto. Following an early Italian goal, they led the semi-final for 82 minutes before defender Karl-Heinz Schellinger equalised at the death.

Schellinger's goal had surprised even the German commentators, but had helped to provide perhaps the greatest period of extra time ever. The West Germans had felt aggrieved by a number of decisions and captain Franz

---

161 Pele, *Pele: The Autobiography* (London: Simon and Schuster, 2008)
162 *Aberdeen Press and Journal*, 15 June 1970

Beckenbauer was forced to play in a sling after dislocating his shoulder towards the end of the game. For the watching Pelé, this had shifted the balance of power in the match.[163] Just four minutes after the restart, Gerd Müller had given the West Germans the lead before Tarcisio Burgnich levelled the scores. Italian striker Luigi Riva then pounced to put the *Azzurri* 3-2 ahead by half-time.

Into the final 15 minutes. In the 110th minute of the game, Müller once again scored to draw level before the Italians went straight down the other end of the pitch to make it 4-3. Gianni Rivera was the hero for Feruccio Valcareggi's side.

The match was revered internationally as both sides left the field exhausted. The *Coventry Evening Telegraph* was particularly appreciative of the efforts as it described the 'sensational match'. It continued to note the reception of the crowds, who rose to their feet and applauded both sides for several minutes. The match was sure to be discussed by lovers of the game long after it was finished.[164]

In Italy, the side were heralded as heroes and belief was felt in abundance for the challenge of Brazil four days later. What occurred, however, was one of the greatest team performances of all time as the *Selecao* overwhelmed them 4-1 in Mexico City. Beckenbauer's men, on the other hand, would use the heartbreak of extra-time defeats in both the 1966 and 1970 World Cups to propel them to greater heights as the tournament came to West German soil in 1974.

The match showed the true beauty of the game and was a real push for attacking football. The rivalry has continued to grow into one of the fiercest in world football. The two sides have subsequently met each other at three World Cups and four European Championships. Victory for Italy in the 1982 World Cup Final and a memorable 2-0 win in Dortmund, 2006 has meant the fixture boasts positive memories for Italians. For

---

163 Pele, *Pele: My Autobiography*
164 *Coventry Evening Telegraph*, 18 June 1970

German fans, the Italian stranglehold means there is no bigger fixture.[165] If there is one game to win, it's this one.

165 Uli Hesse, 'How Italy became Germany's true international rivals', *ESPN* (March 2011) https://www.espn.com/soccer/club/germany/481/blog/post/2838013/how-italy-became-germanys-true-international-rivals

1974–86

26

The FIFA World Cup 1974: East Beats West, Total Football and Johan Cruyff (1974)

Over the course of these 50 moments, many World Cups will undoubtedly feature. There is certainly an argument to be made, though, that 1974 was one of the greatest and most important of them all. Hosted by West Germany (GDR), 16 teams lined up from five different confederations – Australia qualifying for their first-ever FIFA World Cup, Zaire (DR Congo) becoming the first Sub-Saharan African team to qualify, whilst England failed in their attempt to feature (Scotland were the sole representative of the home nations).

The first stunning moment of 1974 came in the group stages – East Germany, drawn in the same group as their Cold War rivals West Germany, pulled off an unexpected victory. The West Germans were one of the pre-tournament favourites, featuring the likes of Paul Breitner, Gerd Müller and captain 'Der Kaiser' Franz Beckenbauer. The side was managed by Helmut Schön, an East German who had learned his trade in the Soviet-occupied east zone before escaping the country in 1950 to further his career and find a better life.[166]

---

166 *The Independent*, 24 February 1996

East Germany (DDR), meanwhile, were appearing in their first (and only) World Cup, playing in West Germany, representing communism against capitalism, and were the clear underdogs. That day, though, at Hamburg's Volksparkstadion, would go down in East German history. With both nations already qualified for the next group round, GDR, with victories over Chile and Australia, DDR with a win against Australia and a draw with Chile, the battle was for pride and to top the group standings. The build-up was fraught with political sensitivities, the players told not to swap shirts on the pitch after the final whistle, whilst 3,000 East Germans were sanctioned to cross the Berlin Wall to attend as spectators but only with heavy policing.[167]

Hans-Jurgen Kreische, East German striker, recalled his excitement that day: 'The players didn't feel any pressure. On the contrary, we were looking forward to comparing ourselves to the West. It was something we repeatedly strived for, but the authorities always prevented.'[168] The match itself was not a thriller, a goalless first half leaving it all to play for in the second 45 minutes. It would be the 77th minute before the deadlock was broken. East German forward Jürgen Sparwasser latched on to a bouncing ball and netted the game's only goal. The DDR had their win 1-0, a monumental moment to stun the watching world.

Kreische remembers that the initial aftermath was actually friendly: 'Following the final whistle all the players swapped shirts, although we didn't do it on the pitch because officially it was forbidden.' He continued, 'We got on very well. We spoke the same language after all.'[169] However, for the West the devastation was clear – Schön, the former East German,

---

167 Clemente A. Lisi, *A History of the World Cup* (Plymouth: Scarecrow Press INC., 2011), p.132

168 Mani Djazmi, 'World Cup whisky and the Cold War: When East & West Germany met', *BBC* (7 March 2019) https://www.bbc.co.uk/sport/football/47456049

169 *Ibid*

was reportedly heartbroken to lose to his old country. British newspapers reported how Beckenbauer brushed Schön aside at a press conference to launch a 'scathing attack' on teammates including winger Jürgen Grabowski and Bayern Munich colleague Uli Hoeness.[170] The loss, though, actually assisted the West Germans, who finished second yet would face an easier second group of Poland, Yugoslavia and Sweden – a group they topped. For DDR, their win left them in a second group of Brazil, Argentina and the Netherlands – finishing third and being sent home across the border.

East Germany would refuse to play West Germany ever again and never met in competitive football; therefore, they claimed a 100 per cent record by the time of reunification in 1990. The East side have been labelled *'Freundschaftsspielweltmeister'* or 'world champions of friendlies' because of the communist nation's tendency to just play non-competitive matches against fellow socialist states.[171] When reunified, the West would boast a far greater international record; however, in the match that mattered in 1974 it was the East who would be able to maintain the bragging rights.

An important World Cup so far, but Total Football is still yet to be mentioned – the Netherlands side that helped change football! Manager Rinus Michels (known as 'The General') was the architect of this revolution, declaring: 'Football is war'.[172] Michels started out as Ajax boss, winning the league four times and a European Cup in 1971. This earned him a move to Spain as Barcelona boss and he would be joined by his country's talisman Johan Cruyff at the Nou Camp in 1973. Those two together would leave an everlasting print on the global stage at the World Cup in 1974; Cruyff won the award for the competition's best player, cementing his super-stardom.

---

170 *Reading Evening Post*, 26 June 1974

171 Markus Hesselmann and Robert Ide, in Alan Tomlinson and Christopher Young (eds.), *German Football: History, Culture, Society* (Abingdon: Routledge, 2006) p.44

172 *The Guardian*, 9 June 2010

Scholten sums up the 'Total Football' style – 'The demanding 4-3-3 system that called on players of exceptional quality to interchange positions and press high up the field, and for all outfield players to be able to participate in attacks. Attack-minded full-backs roamed the flanks and even a "flying" goalkeeper was encouraged to take part in the passage of play.'[173]

This style of football helped the Dutch march through the tournament, topping their initial group with six goals in three matches. The second group stage saw them win their next three ties against Brazil (2-0), East Germany (1-0) and Argentina (4-0). The reward was a place in the final at the Olympiastadion, Munich, where on 7 July 1974 their opponents would be West Germany. They had also stormed their second group stage, recovering from that loss to their Eastern rivals in the first stage. The well-fancied home favourites of West Germany v the incredibly popular Total Footballing Dutch.

Just a minute into the game, before the Germans had even touched the ball, the Netherlands had the lead via a penalty. English referee Jack Taylor pointed to the spot after Cruyff took the ball through the German defence 'like an eel', leaving the opposition 'panting' before being brought down by Hoeness.[174] The Germans did not panic, however – Berti Vogts man-marked Cruyff out of the game and forced the Dutch to play far more defensive football than had been seen during the tournament so far. In the 25th minute Bernd Hölzenbein was fouled in the Dutch penalty area and this allowed Paul Breitner a chance to strike back from the spot – 1-1. The momentum was clearly with the Germans and, after sustained pressure, what turned out to be the game-winning strike was netted by Gerd Müller in the 43rd minute.[175]

173 Berend Scholten, 'Michels – a total footballing legend', *UEFA* (3 March 2005) https://www.uefa.com/insideuefa/about-uefa/history/obituaries/newsid=285010.html?redirectFromOrg=true

174 *Daily Mirror*, 8 July 1974

175 Clemente A. Lisi, *A History of the World Cup*, p.140

The second-half performance saw Total Football return, bringing *Daily Mirror* journalist Frank McGhee to write: 'I'd love to have heard what was said in the Dutch dressing room at half-time to produce such a transformation in mood, style and approach.' He reported that even with the strength of the German side, 'they looked at times as though they must be swamped by an orange tide'.[176] Johan Neeskens spurned a number of good chances, as did Cruyff, whilst Breitner and Beckenbauer put in sterling displays to help maintain West Germany's lead. As the full-time whistle blew, the Germans could begin to celebrate a famous victory at their home World Cup. For the Dutch, hearts were broken and to this day it is still considered an opportunity missed for Michels's magnificent 'Oranje'.

---

176 *Daily Mirror*, 8 July 1974

27

England's European Cup Dominance (1977–84)

As Moment 19 remembered, Real Madrid dominated the first years of the European Cup by winning the first five tournaments. However, by 1977 the winners had been spread throughout Europe – Spain with six (all Real), Italy with four (Milan two, Internazionale two), Netherlands four (Feyenoord one and Ajax three), West Germany three (all Bayern Munich), Portugal two (both Benfica), Scotland one (Celtic) and England just one (Manchester United). 1977, though, marked a change in the tide in favour of the English, clubs from England winning seven out of the next eight European Cups.

The first of those was Liverpool in the Stadio Olimpico in Rome. West German side Borussia Mönchengladbach were hoping to add another title to the German list of winners, but the Reds stood in their way. With both sides appearing in their first European Cup Final, it would be Bob Paisley's men who would lift the trophy after 90 minutes. The *Daily Mirror* labelled retiring defender Tommy Smith and Hamburg-bound forward Kevin Keegan as 'heroes' on an 'unforgettable night' in Italy. Smith scored his first of the season, with Terry McDermott and Phil Neal also helping seal the 3-1 victory and bring sheer delight to Merseyside.[177]

---

177 *Daily Mirror*, 26 May 1977

The very next year Liverpool would again assert their continental dominance and reach the European Cup Final, this time at Wembley Stadium. Club Brugge of Belgium were tasked with seizing the trophy from the Reds, but it was Liverpool's 'tartan twosome' who opened up the Belgian defences. Scotsman Graeme Souness's 'artistry' in midfield played in compatriot Kenny Dalglish, who sealed the match in the 64th minute with a delightful dink over the Brugge keeper.[178] Liverpool were back-to-back champions of Europe!

1979's final saw a different English power step up to the plate – Brian Clough's Nottingham Forest. Having beaten defending champions Liverpool 2-0 on aggregate in the first round, denying the Merseysiders a shot at a hat-trick, Malmö would be Forest's final opposition. The Olympiastadion in Munich hosted what would become the greatest day in Forest's history, Swedish outfit Malmö unexpectedly reaching the final on 30 May via a fairly kind route to Germany. Nottingham Forest's team, containing just British players, were not considered a mighty side themselves but dominated the proceedings as Malmö kept things tight. The winner would come thanks to a Trevor Francis goal in first-half injury time, Britain's first million pound player helping pay back some of his price tag with an excellent display in Germany.[179] Delirium ensued at full time – Forest were European champions!

The following year Forest were handed a kind run of ties as they reached the final a second time. Their run saw them beat Leo Beenhakker's Dutch champions Ajax 2-1 on aggregate in the semis in their most difficult fixture of the competition. Hamburg of Germany, meanwhile, beat Real Madrid 5-1 in the second leg of their semi-final to win 5-3 on aggregate, preventing *Los Blancos* a European Cup shot at their home stadium, the Santiago Bernabéu. On 28 May 1980 it would be Forest's keeper who helped them defend their

---

178 *Liverpool Echo*, 11 May 1978
179 *Birmingham Evening Post*, 31 May 1979

crown, 'an outstanding display of goalkeeping' frustrating an exciting Hamburg side.[180] At the other end of the pitch, it was Scottish winger John Robertson who netted the only goal in the 20th minute to seal yet another English success. Forest, like Liverpool, had done it twice in a row!

So, four in four years for the English First Division; what would 1981 hold? More of the same! This time it would be Liverpool who returned to the top of the tree. The Reds had marched comfortably through the earlier rounds but needed the away-goals rule via Ray Kennedy to see off Bayern Munich in the semi-finals that season. Real Madrid had this year made it to the final in Paris, bettering their finish of the previous one. However, the might of Bob Paisley's men saw them disappointed as Real continued their 15-year European Cup dry run. Given an entertainment rating of just 3/5 by the *Liverpool Echo*, the tense occasion was only separated by left-back Alan Kennedy's late winner.[181] The Englishman put his name in the history books and secured a third trophy for Merseyside, ending its loan to Nottingham.

The final British winner in this remarkable streak was Aston Villa in 1982, again the greatest night in the club's history. Villa were led by manager Tony Barton, who had only been in the post since February 1982. They would face off against European heavyweights Bayern Munich in Rotterdam, Holland – a squad containing the likes of captain Paul Breitner and the talented Karl-Heinz Rummenigge. Like the previous four finals, the game finished 1-0, with a single strike from Peter Withe winning the tie. Another goalkeeper could claim hero status, though, this time Nigel Spink. The reserve stopper had only previously featured once for Villa but with first-choice Jimmy Rimmer coming off injured just ten minutes into the game, Spink stepped up to save the day for the Midlands club and shared his disbelief: 'I don't believe it, I have only played

---

180 *Newcastle Journal*, 29 May 1980

181 *Liverpool Echo*, 28 May 1981

two matches and I am here with a European Cup winners' medal!'[182] It was now five in a row and Europe were in the palm of England's hand!

It would be Hamburg that halted this English juggernaut. The West Germans faced Italians Juventus in the 1983 Athens final, Juve having put defending champions Villa out in the quarter-finals. The other English representative, Liverpool, were eliminated by Polish club Widzew Łódź 4-3 on aggregate, also in the quarter-finals.

The fallow year was only to last one season, however, as Liverpool hit back in 1983/84. Another final for the Reds lined them up against AS Roma, who were seeking a first Italian trophy since 1969. Liverpool had scored 15 and conceded just two en route to the Stadio Olympico – Roma, meanwhile, had ended Dundee United's hopes of a final place with a 3-2 aggregate win. Roma had the advantage of playing the European Cup Final at home but the game ended 1-1 after 90 minutes. Extra time could not separate the sides and penalties would be required; Phil Neal, Graeme Souness, Ian Rush and Alan Kennedy all netted and Anfield would have a familiar trophy in its cabinet to join the 'truly remarkable collection of silverware' (the First Division title and the Milk Cup).[183]

This period is without doubt English football's European heyday, the constant continental dominance a source of pride for the British Isles. The unmatched level of consistency from First Division teams looked set to continue in 1985 – but disaster would strike for English clubs and the footballing world … More on that in Moment 29.

---

182 *Belfast Telegraph*, 27 May 1982
183 *Liverpool Echo*, 31 May 1984

28

Bradford City Stadium Fire (1985)

Our next two moments are terribly sad but very important nonetheless. Firstly, the Bradford Stadium Fire of 1985. Bradford City played (and still play) their home matches at Valley Parade. The stadium itself was opened in 1886, as the home of Manningham rugby club until 1903, when Manningham changed sports – rugby became association football and the name became Bradford City.

On 11 May 1985, Bradford hosted Lincoln City. Valley Parade was in a party atmosphere as Bradford were to be presented with the Third Division trophy. With the game at 0-0, in the 40th minute disaster struck. A fan, believed to be an Australian visitor, tried to stub out his cigarette on the wooden planks of the stand. Unfortunately the cigarette fell through the hole in the slats to the ground below.[184] The wood and congregated rubbish made for perfect tinder – the fire took hold.

Fans rushed for fire extinguishers, but after being unable to find any the fire brigade were called. This call happened at just 3.43pm, three minutes after the fire began, but it was too late. The referee was informed and half-time was called as fans raced on to the pitch for safety. However, it was too late for 56 individuals who tragically lost their lives in the ensuing

---

184 *The Telegraph*, 12 May 2015

inferno and choking smoke; 265 others also suffered injuries in an event that stunned the footballing world.

Off-duty detective Michael Blanchfield spoke about the horror of that day: 'When I first saw it, it was a pale grey wisp or puff of smoke and what appeared to be a very minor fire.' However, the fire took hold quickly and Blanchfield describes the panic that ensued in Valley Parade: 'When we got into the street we were engulfed in thick choking black smoke. Only about four minutes after leaving our seats the place was engulfed in flames.'[185]

The dreadful scenes were captured by TV cameras and the commentator that day, John Helm, had the awful task of keeping talking whilst the fire unfolded before his, and the watching public's, eyes. 'Oh, the poor man, the poor man' – Helm's voice displayed his emotions as a man was engulfed by the flames, Helm remembering, 'I was conscious of choosing my words very carefully and at the same time trying to tell people exactly what was going on.'[186] For Helm the scenes have been too harrowing to ever rewatch, but they provided valuable evidence for investigation work, as well as future fire emergency training.

The immediate aftermath brought an immense outpouring of grief and the public responded. The Bradford Disaster Appeal raised over £3.5m, a campaign that included a rematch of the 1966 World Cup Final with England and Germany's original line-ups turning out in support.[187] Following Bradford, wider questions were asked about the safety at UK football grounds. The government ordered the Popplewell Report, but sadly football was not in a good place in 1985. The game was in the midst of its 'hooligan problem', with mindless fans causing trouble up and down the country. Back in 1980, Nicholas Keith, sports editor of *The Times*, had written: 'If we

---

185 *Reading Evening Post*, 25 July 1985
186 *Yorkshire Post*, 6 May 2015
187 *The Guardian*, 29 July 1985

do not [do something] there is a real danger that football will die for lack of support, because only thugs will go to watch it ... Football is sick, it may be terminal.'[188]

Part of the response to hooliganism had been safety fencing to separate home and away supporters – ultimately this led to some fans at Bradford being trapped from escape. The report also found that the stand in question had previously been condemned for redevelopment but lack of club finances had prevented this. Newspapers continued to criticise football, labelling it 'a slum sport, played in slum stadiums, increasingly watched by slum people who deter decent folk from turning up.'[189]

Action was needed to salvage the game, but Johnes writes how the government often excluded sport from legislation, meaning by the middle of the decade football had far more issues than just hooliganism, as stadium safety had become a major concern for match-goers. The Popplewell Report made a number of recommendations after Bradford, but historians believe it was affected by the hooliganism that swirled in Britain. This led to it avoiding some of the stadium safety concerns that would lead to problems in future disasters: 'Much good sense came out of the report but it was responded to and shaped by the question of hooliganism rather than safety.'[190]

Bradford's Valley Parade disaster was a tragic accident in 1985, one not caused by hooliganism, but the worst disaster in the history of the Football League was undoubtedly another hammer blow to a sport that was seen to be 'terminally ill'.

---

188 *The Times*, 19 September 1980

189 *The Sunday Times*, 19 May 1985

190 Martin Johnes, in Paul Darby, Martin Johnes and Gavin Mellor, (eds), *Soccer and Disaster* (London: Routledge, 2005) p.19

29

Heysel Stadium Disaster (1985)

With British football stunned by what happened in Bradford on 11 May 1985, more terrible scenes were to come just days later. Moment 27 recorded the dominance of English clubs in the European Cup from 1977–1984, its football on the pitch arguably at its greatest-ever peak. However, Moment 28 saw how the sport had a hooliganism problem off the field. Whilst Bradford was not caused by hooliganism, the Heysel Disaster, on 29 May 1985, was a result of the tensions fans brought to watching the beautiful game.

The 1985 European Cup had seen reigning champions Liverpool march to the final once again. Lech Poznań, Benfica, Austria Wien and Panathinaikos had been swept aside by the Reds whilst their Italian opponents Juventus had seen off Ilves, Grasshoppers, Sparta Prague and Bordeaux. The final was to be hosted by Heysel Stadium in Brussels, Belgium, on 29 May 1985 in front of 58,000 fans.

The game was due to kick off at 8pm local time, but around 7pm things turned sour. Liverpool and Juventus supporters behind one of the goals, separated by the matter of a few metres and a limp, chain link fence, clashed. The mentality is perhaps best summarised by the attitude of a Cardiff fan: 'That's what it is all about. You've to get in their end and take it.'[191] Stones

---

191 Richard Holt, *Sport and the British: A Modern History* (Oxford: Oxford University, 1989) p.330

were thrown as well as pieces of the dilapidated stand itself. The violence got more and more intense and Liverpool fans ended up in a Juventus section of the stand. Sadly, thousands of fans were caught up in the madness and confusion that this created and a wall collapsed.

The death toll, due to suffocation and crushing, amounted to 39 people: 32 Italians (the youngest of whom was 11), four Belgians, two French and one fan was from Northern Ireland. Police and medical staff rushed to treat the injured; it is believed that this amounted to 600+.[192] The reaction of the Juventus fans at the other end of the pitch was to rush the Liverpool fans in anger as the emergency services sought calm. No stretchers were available and so victims were carried out on fences and advertising hoardings.[193]

Unbelievably, after the authorities had some level of calm, it was decided that it was better to play the European Cup Final after all. This decision is a staggering one and Juventus went on to win the tie 1-0, Michel Platini netting a penalty to seal victory and their first-ever European Cup. 1985 would not be remembered for its football though – 1985 marked a year that hooliganism became the wretch of the beautiful game.

The British press were immediate and extreme in their reaction. Blame was placed on the shoulders of the policing and crowd control that night, whilst Heysel Stadium was criticised as an inadequate facility to host a major cup final. However, the *Liverpool Echo* was clearer in who it blamed for the disaster: 'The behaviour of thousands of Liverpool and Turin supporters, with the Merseysiders in the majority, turned the evening into one of sheer horror.'[194] FA chairman Bert Millichip was disgusted by the events too: 'The scale of this tragedy is so depressing it is beyond belief. I feel entirely

---

192 *Liverpool Echo*, 23 May 2015

193 Bryon Butler, *The Football League: The First 100 Years* (Guildford: Colour Library Books Ltd., 1988)

194 *Liverpool Echo*, 30 May 1985

helpless and completely frustrated as to what action can be taken, if indeed the game of football can survive at all.'[195]

Hooliganism had long been the scourge of the British game, fans turning their back on the sport, further allowing the hooligans to seize control of football. Now, though, Heysel had opened the eyes of the wider public, including hooligans themselves. Andy Nicholls, an Everton hooligan, was in Brussels that night and describes his emotions: 'It was horrible and I felt sick. It could have been anybody dying, your dad or even your kids. It was not what my notion of football hooliganism was about.'[196] The need for a quick response was clear. With the beautiful game in Britain on the verge of collapse, the demand was that 'the lunatic fringe must be weeded out … and weeded out quickly'.[197]

The punishment handed out for English clubs was severe. Prime Minister Margaret Thatcher sought to withdraw English clubs from European competition: 'We have to get the game cleaned up from this hooliganism at home and then perhaps we shall be able to go overseas again.'[198] Liverpool withdrew from the UEFA Cup (for which they had qualified for 1985/86), whilst the FA decided that all English clubs would be withdrawn from European competition. UEFA then took the decision to extend this exile with an indefinite ban of English clubs. Clubs such as Everton, Wimbledon and Coventry City missed their chance at European Cup and Cup Winners' Cup football, whilst the likes of Southampton, Norwich City, Luton Town and Derby County missed out on their UEFA Cup spots.

The ban continued until April 1990 – 1990/91 being the first season to allow the re-introduction of English clubs.

---

195 *Daily Mirror*, 31 May 1985

196 Andy Nicholls, *Scally* (Preston: Milo Books, 2004) pp.178-86

197 *Liverpool Echo*, 30 May 1985

198 Jon Carter, 'Rewind: The Heysel aftermath', *ESPN* (1 June 2011) https://www.espn.co.uk/football/columns/story/_/id/925085/rewind:-the-heysel-aftermath-in-1985.

Liverpool, who had a further suspension, would see that lifted for the 1991/92 campaign.

Historian Taylor writes how English football was 'ostracised and isolated from Europe and the world'.[199] Holt, writing in 1989 whilst hooliganism continued, adds that the actions that night emphasised the 'fatal risks being run each week in stadia where large and rowdy confrontations of young spectators take place'.[200] Punishments were eventually handed out to some supporters who were deemed responsible for causing involuntary manslaughter as well as other offences. On 28 April 1989, following a protracted trial, 14 Liverpool fans were found guilty and sentenced to three years in prison (18 months of which were suspended), whilst ten other defendants were cleared of the charges they faced.[201]

The shameful events of Heysel began to change the picture of hooliganism as the FA declared: 'It is up to English football to put its house in order, to ensure that this totally unacceptable behaviour of English supporters at home and abroad becomes a thing of the past.'[202] However, it is still horrendous to think that it took the heartbreak of the Heysel Disaster and the struggle of the following years, ending with Hillsborough in 1989, to reclaim football for the everyday fan, not the 'thug'.

199 Matthew Taylor, *The Association Game* (London: Routledge, 2008) p.319
200 Richard Holt, *Sport and the British: A Modern History*, p.329
201 *Liverpool Echo*, 23 May 2015
202 *Aberdeen Evening Express*, 31 May 1985

30

The Hand of God and the Goal of the Century (1986)

This book of 50 moments will undoubtedly cause debates: What is the greatest moment? What is the most important moment? But we do think that this moment here is probably the most famous. Even those who don't profess to love the beautiful game know all about 'The Hand of God', the day on which Diego Maradona broke English hearts with two goals in Mexico's 1986 World Cup.

This was the second time Mexico had the privilege of having a World Cup come to town. The 1970 tournament was dominated by Pelé's Brazil and their wonder team; this time, Mexico were 'prepared to anoint his successor'.[203] Twenty-four countries took their place in June 1986: Northern Ireland, Scotland and England amongst the 14 UEFA representatives, along with defending champions Italy. Sadly for both Northern Ireland and Scotland, their contribution would finish in the group stages, neither side managing a win as they secured just a draw each in group D and E.

Prior to the World Cup, in 1982, international tensions had seen Argentina and Britain go to war over the Falkland Islands in the south of the Atlantic Ocean. The British territory had

---

203 Clemente A. Lisi, *A History of the World Cup*, p.190

long been disputed, with Argentina claiming rights over it, but the citizens themselves declaring their allegiance to the UK. Britain would win that war but lose 255 lives in the process, Argentina losing 649 of their troops, many thousands more wounded for both nations.

This tension would not have totally disappeared by the time 1986's World Cup came around, fans from both sides clashing in the streets of Mexico City. FA secretary Ted Croker, already smarting from the damaging Heysel Disaster, longed for sport and politics to be kept separate. Croker remarked: 'Sport is sport and politics is politics', claiming that their upcoming quarter-final game was 'a wonderful opportunity to build a bridge between our two countries'.[204]

En route to the last eight, Argentina had topped their group, winning twice and drawing once – Real Madrid forward Jorge Valdano netting three of their six goals. England, meanwhile, had come second in their group – winning, drawing and losing once (to Portugal, Morocco and Poland respectively). Argentina had then seen off fellow South Americans Uruguay 1-0 in their last-16 match, an 'inspired' Diego Maradona proving why he was the 'world's most valuable player'[205] before (future Bangor City manager) Pedro Pasculli secured the winner. England brushed aside Paraguay 3-0 in their match, with goals coming from a Gary Lineker brace and a Peter Beardsley strike from close range.

This set up a mouth-watering quarter-final tie: Argentina versus England. Argentina – featuring Napoli (and former Barcelona) superstar Maradona as captain, England with goalkeeper Peter Shilton as their captain and led by the goals of Lineker (who would finish as the Golden Boot at the end of the tournament). Both managers played down the political ill feeling pre-game, Argentina's Carlos Bilardo writing, 'We have come here to play soccer and nothing else,' whilst

---

204 *Irish Independent*, 20 June 1986
205 *Aberdeen Press and Journal*, 17 June 1986

England's Bobby Robson was clear in his press conference: 'I'm a football manager and not a politician, so don't ask me those kind of questions.'[206]

So to the game itself ... The first half was a fairly tight affair, with England under pressure but holding out to take it to the break at 0-0. However, the game would come to life in the second 45 and lead to two unforgettable moments in football history. Firstly, in the 51st minute Maradona picked the ball up 40 yards out in the centre of the pitch. After beating three men on his advance to the penalty area and attempting a one-two with team-mate Valdano, the ball was deflected backwards and into the air by England midfielder Steve Hodge. Maradona, who had continued his run into the box, leapt up with keeper Peter Shilton and seemed to beat him to the ball with his head – 1-0.

England, though, were immediately incensed, and replays showed that Maradona had used his hand to 'punch' the ball into the back of the net. Newspapers highlighted the outrage back home, describing how England were 'cheated'[207] by the 'killer punch'.[208] The 5ft 4in magician showed no remorse afterwards, saying famously that the goal was scored 'a little with the head of Maradona and a little with the hand of God'.[209] Thus, the 'hand of god' was born.

Just four minutes later, in the 55th minute, Maradona would put the game beyond the English, the 'Goal of the Century' making this one of the most famous games in the history of the sport. Maradona picked the ball up in his own half and started his rush to goal; the 60 yards taking him just ten seconds as he beat four men, including Terry Butcher twice! Maradona then dribbled the ball past the helpless goalkeeper Peter Shilton to finish off this stunning piece of

---

206 *Staffordshire Sentinel*, 19 June 1986

207 *Staffordshire Sentinel*, 23 June 1986

208 *Sandwell Evening Mail*, 23 June 1986

209 Dan Walker, *Dan Walker's Football Thronkersaurus: Football's Finest Tales* (London: Simon & Schuster UK Ltd., 2014) p.184

artistry. I can't really do it justice, so recommend you search the goal online (best viewed with superb South American commentary by Víctor Hugo Morales)!

Lineker would net for England in the 81st minute to take his tournament tally to six, but Argentina would take the 2-1 victory to set up a semi-final with Belgium. Maradona would strike twice again to secure a place in the final, their opponents, West Germany, seeing off the French in their semi-final.

The Estadio Azteca was packed with almost 115,000 spectators on 29 June 1986, a gripping final anticipated. Argentina took a 2-0 lead and seemingly were heading for their second world title, but Karl-Heinz Rummenigge's 74th-minute strike was followed by Rudi Völler's 80th-minute header – did extra time loom? Just three minutes after the scores were levelled, Independiente's attacking midfielder Jorge Burruchaga was found by Maradona and he stepped up to win the game for Argentina.

Argentina were World Cup champions, Maradona was hated by many yet adored by many more! As Lisi puts it: 'What he could do with a mere touch of the ball was comparable to what Frank Sinatra did with a microphone and Pablo Picasso with a paintbrush.'[210]

---

210 Clemente A. Lisi, *A History of the World Cup*, pp.214-15

1986–92

31

Alex Ferguson Joins Manchester United (1986)

Today, there are a wealth of names synonymous with Manchester United; Bobby Charlton, George Best and Ryan Giggs to name but three. There is, however, one which arguably upstages even these three legends of the modern game. That name is, of course, Sir Alex Ferguson. Despite a relative lack of success in recent years, the past two decades were truly dominated by Ferguson's United. Playing a blend of attacking football with defensive solidity, the side were relatively unbeatable on their day. What is perhaps the most surprising is where the club were prior to his arrival.

To fully grasp the magnitude of the task Ferguson faced as he entered Old Trafford, it is important to take a closer look at United's biggest rivals, Liverpool. The 1970s and 1980s had been dominated by the Merseyside club. Indeed, under the guidance of influential managers Bill Shankly, Bob Paisley, Joe Fagan and Kenny Dalglish, the Reds had swept aside all that was in front of them.

Between 1970 and 1986, Liverpool had won the league nine times as well as the European Cup on four occasions. Together with league success for rivals Everton in 1985, there seemed to be no way of stopping the Merseyside dominance of English football.

Manchester United had seen only minor success in the same period. The days of Charlton, Best and the Busby Babes were long gone, and despite boasting a squad with talented players like Bryan Robson and Mark Hughes, United had only three FA Cups to their name since 1968. The 1985/86 season had started off successfully as the club had won 13 of their first 15 league matches. United had led the table until February, but then a series of disappointing results and an injury to Robson saw them fall behind Everton.

Across Stanley Park, Liverpool had suffered through a gruelling winter, but recovered under player-manager Kenny Dalglish to win 11 of their last 12 games and pinch the league from the blue half of Merseyside. What was to further compound the misery in Manchester was Liverpool's FA Cup triumph at Wembley, once more at Everton's expense. The Reds were well and truly on their perch and there was little chance of them falling off. For many fans and commentators, the scouse supremacy was too much to take. Jimmy Greaves went as far as saying, 'I wish they'd cut Merseyside off from the rest of the country, float it out into the Irish Sea ... so all the other clubs have a chance of winning something!'[211]

The following season, United had suffered a terrible slump in form. Losing six of their opening eight games and a third-round League Cup exit at the hands of Southampton meant Atkinson's days were over. In stepped Alex Ferguson. As manager of Scottish club Aberdeen, Ferguson enjoyed impressive success – winning three Scottish Leagues, four Scottish Cups and even the Cup Winners' Cup in 1983. For United, surely he could be the man to bring silverware to the club on a consistent basis.

Ferguson had admired former Liverpool manager Bill Shankly. Both from similar backgrounds, they knew that their respective side's on-field pitfalls could only be fixed through

---

211 Jimmy Greaves in Simon Hart, *Here We Go: Everton in the 1980s: The Players' Stories* (Liverpool, deCoubertin, 2014)

an overhaul of more than just the starting XI. However, the start to his reign at Old Trafford was anything but smooth. Citing the poor fitness of many first team players like Bryan Robson and Norman Whiteside, he instigated an overhaul of the club's training methods and off-the-pitch antics. Up until his arrival, United's image had been tarnished by reports of players drinking heavily with a 'docker's bar mentality'.[212]

For Ferguson, the training ground became 'sacrosanct'. It became a place of consistency, where standards never dropped. In that way, after a bad game, players could get back to routine straight away, with the full support and expertise of the staff.[213] Results on the pitch took a while to improve. The inconsistency in performance they had shown under Ron Atkinson continued – 11th, second, 11th and 13th were not the rankings of champions, and in 1990 Ferguson's job was on the line. Following eight league games without a win, only victory over Forest in the cup would be enough for 'Fergie' to remain at the helm. A Mark Robins goal in the 56th minute provided the win the Red Devils needed. At the end of the season, United won the FA Cup, beating Crystal Palace at Wembley.

United's board had been rewarded for sticking by their man. In the modern game, there is little chance a manager would be able to survive at Old Trafford following mid-table finishes. In Ferguson, however, there was something else. Thirteen Premier Leagues, two European Cups, five FA Cups and four League Cups later, his legacy is unbeatable. The recent slump in fortunes for United ever since Ferguson's departure are further testament to his success. With no Premier League title since 2012/13 (Ferguson's final season), the club is well and truly in need of history repeating itself.

---

212 Paul McGrath, *Back From The Brink: The Autobiography* (London: Arrow, 2006) p.164

213 Sir Alex Ferguson, *My Autobiography* (London: Hodder and Stoughton, 2013)

32

The Hillsborough Disaster (1989)

As we have already seen in this list, despite the brilliance and identity football can bring, tragedy is never far away. In 1989 and the years that followed, the game was to see one of its saddest episodes. The scale and legacy left by the Hillsborough disaster is perhaps clearest from the fact that criminal prosecutions are still taking place 30 years after the tragedy. Due to this, we are restricted from what we can and can't write in this edition.

Nevertheless, it would be remiss to exclude such a poignant moment. The match was an FA Cup semi-final tie between Liverpool and Nottingham Forest. Hillsborough's large capacity meant it became a popular 'neutral' ground to host the fixture. Liverpool supporters were to take up the Leppings Lane end of the ground, which in the years previous had been the scene of a number of crushes. In the 1981 semi-final between Tottenham and Wolves, serious overcrowding had led to injuries to over 30 people. In 1987 a similar scenario occurred during the semi-final fixture between Coventry and Leeds, before the problem resurfaced the following year with Liverpool in 1988.

Perhaps key to the overcrowding issue at Hillsborough was the introduction of large metal fences designed to keep supporters from invading the pitch. Such measures were commonplace in English football following two decades of hooliganism spoiling the game. Prior to the semi-final in 1989, Liverpool had lodged a complaint about the suitability of Hillsborough due to its poor track record and cramped conditions. Nevertheless, the stadium was chosen once again to host one of the football calendar's most popular ties.

Despite a drop in average attendances in the English Football League since the 1970s, the FA Cup semi-final was still a game most fans wanted to attend. A large number of spectators arrived in Sheffield for the match on 15 April looking forward to an exciting game. Over 24,000 Liverpool fans were filtered through a single entrance into the turnstiles. Due to the segregation of supporters at the game, further turnstiles were closed off to avoid confrontation between fans. It appeared that instead of putting crowd safety first, the eradication of potential hooliganism was more important.

Liverpool fans were slowly making their way into the ground as kick-off approached. Indeed, for many it seemed that the stand was almost empty with just ten minutes until the game started. After declining calls to delay the start of the game and to quicken the flow of spectators into the ground, it was decided by police to open an exit gate. This way, Liverpool fans could freely enter into the Leppings Lane end without delay. Two further gates were opened around the turnstiles and as a result two of the pens began to fill up quickly. The supporters at the front of the pens were beginning to be crushed as the weight of fans grew and grew.

The crush would claim the lives of 96 Liverpool fans in total. The match was abandoned after just six minutes as steel fences were broken under the sheer weight of the crush. Fans spilled and escaped on to the pitch, using advertising hoardings as makeshift stretchers for their friends, family and fellow Liverpool fans. Over 700 further supporters were injured. By the time ambulances began to arrive at Hillsborough, much of the damage and devastation had already taken place.

Following the tragedy, public opinion was mixed. Indeed, many were influenced by the tabloid press, who it seemed were more intent on headlines and selling copies of their papers. *The Sun* ran with the headline 'The Truth', which contained fabricated stories about the behaviour of Liverpool fans, pinning the blame entirely on them. Following the Heysel tragedy in 1985 and with hooliganism still rife within English football, for many this story seemed plausible. For those at the stadium and for the families of the 96, such stories were clearly not true.

On the pitch, the match would be replayed despite objections from some supporters. Liverpool beat Forest 3-1 at Old Trafford and perhaps fittingly met Everton in the final at Wembley. In Merseyside, it was not uncommon for families to have both reds and blues, with many Everton fans personally impacted by the tragedy at Hillsborough. Liverpool went on to win the final 3-2 following an enthralling match which saw three goals in extra time. Ian Rush was the hero with his late winner. Both sides wore black armbands during the match and fans were united in their grief. The result offered some respite for those affected but was of no real importance. For the families of the 96, the long fight for justice was about to begin.

Perhaps the defining moment came at the 25th anniversary service of the tragedy at Anfield. Stepping forward to the microphone to address the thousands of fans and families of the victims was Labour MP Andy Burnham. Burnham began with a speech repeating the same words many had heard for the past quarter of a century. Empty words which he clearly did not believe in. Interrupted by a cacophony of chants singing 'Justice for the 96', Burnham stopped and listened. The campaign was reignited, the debate was reopened and the truth was to be revealed. In September 2012 the Hillsborough Independent Panel found that Liverpool fans were in no way to blame for what happened. This would lead to public apologies from *The Sun*, the House of Commons and others who had made supporters scapegoats for the disaster.

33

Johan Cruyff's Dream Team (1992)

In 1974 we saw perhaps the greatest-ever international team to not win a major tournament – Holland. Their star man was Ajax's Johan Cruyff – who, with his attacking flair and guile, amazed spectators and television audiences alike. The total football of the Dutch had helped innovative and attacking tactics to thrive after decades of *catenaccio* dominance. Following a successful stint at Spanish giants Barcelona from 1973–78, it was only natural that the Dutch magician would eventually manage the club. In 1988 Cruyff became manager of the Catalans.

In the 1980s, Barcelona were in turmoil. With only two La Liga titles in 28 years and political tensions from within the club leading to unrest, the club needed something or someone to change their fortunes. On the other hand, their biggest rivals, Real Madrid, had been successful throughout the decade. Spearheaded by the attacking brilliance of Emilio Butragueno, Madrid had won the league five times and consecutive UEFA Cups in 1985 and 1986. Key to the success of Real was its promotion of youth. The aforementioned Butragueno, together with Sanchis, Michel, Vazquez and Pardeza, seemed to be an unstoppable force. For many the cultural rebirth of the side had echoed Spain's own cultural revolution following the death of Franco in 1975.[214]

---

214 Sid Lowe, *Fear and Loathing in La Liga: Barcelona vs Real Madrid* (London: Random House, 2013) pp.247-8

Barcelona would need a similar change in fortunes in order to compete at the highest level. The club had been littered with problems and the good old days were seemingly gone. A fractured institution, Barcelona had problems off the pitch as well as on it. Perhaps the most notable was the Hesperia Mutiny. Club president Jose Luis Nunez had become immensely unpopular due to his dictatorial style of management. Players and staff rallied against the president at the Hesperia Hotel and called for his resignation. Club unity was seemingly dead.

Furthermore, the *Boixos Nois* casuals group had caused a wealth of issues in the stands, leading to a number of unseemly incidents amongst supporters of the *Blaugrana*.[215] In the season prior to Cruyff's appointment, Barca had finished sixth, 23 points behind winners Real Madrid. Cruyff had been in charge of his former club, Ajax, when the call came from Barcelona. A populist move from Nunez, Cruyff was to be the man to reinvigorate the club.

In the late 1970s, the *Blaugrana* opened their youth academy, La Masia. Cruyff, who, as a player, had seen the impact youth players could have on the first team, began to utilise this resource. His sides would have a mix of home-grown Spaniards and other world-class signings. Perhaps the most recognisable of the La Masia academy was Pep Guardiola, given his debut in 1990. Alongside the current Manchester City manager were superstars like Ronald Koeman, Hristo Stoichkov and Michael Laudrup.

By focussing on the youth teams at La Masia, Cruyff was able to create a unique and genuine football culture at the Camp Nou. Spanish football in the early 1990s was to be dominated by the Catalan club. Winning four successive La Ligas (1991–94), the pendulum had well and truly swung in their favour. Cruyff's work had gone deeper than just who to

---

215 Richard Fitzpatrick, *El Clasico: Barcelona v Real Madrid: Football's Greatest Rivalry* (London: Bloomsbury, 2012) p.57

pick in his starting XI. Indeed, he had worked tirelessly to change the mentality and help the club develop a backbone.[216] Cruyff would develop his side to play attractive football, yet they were also incredibly hard to play against.

The adoption of a 3-4-3 formation was an adaptation of his playing days in Rinus Michels's 4-3-3. What was more, Cruyff was quick to help disseminate his new, radical approach throughout the club. Passing and possession were promoted to stifle and tire the opposition. Barcelona 'B' and the various youth teams would all deploy the 3-4-3. In that way, players in La Masia could immediately step into the first team. Incredibly, Cruyff gave first-team debuts to 32 graduates in just seven seasons.[217]

Their peak came in 1992. Following two successive league titles, a Cup Winners' Cup and Copa Del Rey, Cruyff's team reached the European Cup Final at Wembley. Meeting them there was Italian side Sampdoria. Barcelona's XI was a testament to the work of the manager – once more it featured a youthful Spanish presence alongside the European and South American talents. Despite the score being locked at 0-0 at full time, Ronald Koeman's goal gave the side victory in the 112th minute. The missing trophy in the Nou Camp cabinet was finally delivered.

We cannot underestimate the influence that Johan Cruyff has had on the game we watch today. One of Cruyff's disciples, Pep Guardiola, owes much of his success to the tactical and club-wide revolution inspired by the Dutchman. In the modern-day Barcelona side, success has often come from the promotion of youth. In 2013 Tito Villanova became the first coach to field 11 graduates from the La Masia academy. Cruyff's legacy goes way beyond Barcelona, however. The

216 Graham Hunter, *Barca: The Making of the Greatest Team in the World* (Backpage, 2012) p.132

217 Andrew Murray, 'How Johan Cruyff reinvented modern football at Barcelona', *FourFourTwo* (1 May 2019) https://www.fourfourtwo.com/features/how-johan-cruyff-reinvented-modern-football-barcelona

1990s and 2000s were dominated by a Manchester United side intent on fielding homegrown players. Johan Cruyff, who died in 2016, will never be forgotten.

34

Denmark Conquer Europe (1992)

Everyone loves an underdog story. Some of the finest moments in the history of sport have been through the actions of the unfancied underachievers. Be it the 1980 Miracle on Ice, Goran Ivanišević's wildcard win at Wimbledon in 2000 or the multitude of lower league upsets in the FA Cup, these moments have given hope and belief to the millions who watched. 1992 was to be no different as Denmark won the European Championships. What was even more astounding is that the side, coached by Richard Møller Nielsen, didn't even qualify for the tournament.

At the turn of the decade, Europe was undergoing immense change, perhaps its most significant since the end of the Second World War. The collapse of the USSR and its communist doctrine had led to a series of revolutions across the continent. In Poland, Czechoslovakia, Hungary and Yugoslavia, the 'Iron Curtain' came down and borders began to be altered to suit the ethnic populations.

Although in many of the nations the protests were peaceful, the same couldn't be said in Yugoslavia. A rise in nationalistic values in the separate republics led to increasing tensions. Declarations of independence in each of the states led to an outbreak of war within the country. Yugoslavia had, in fact, as a footballing nation, qualified for the 1992 European Championships. Their status in the tournament was thrown into doubt as a result of the wars and eventually they were removed. But who to replace them?

In stepped the Danes. Denmark had finished as runners-up to Yugoslavia in qualifying and were the natural replacements. The Scandinavian nation were given just one week to prepare a squad to compete in neighbouring Sweden. Boasting quality players like Peter Schmeichel and the Laudrup brothers, Brian and Michael, Denmark would surely have enough to compete with the best Europe had to offer.

But Michael wouldn't join the squad. During the qualification campaign, he had fallen out with Møller Nielsen over his early substitution against Northern Ireland with the score at 1-1.[218] Defeat in Yugoslavia was the final act for Michael Laudrup under Nielsen. Laudrup had been the focal point of the great Barcelona side under Johan Cruyff and the weight of responsibility and different ways of playing ultimately proved too much. Retiring from international duty at the age of 26, the Danes had lost their talisman.

In the group stages, they had fought to earn a creditable draw against World Cup semi-finalists England, before losing to bitter rivals Sweden. In the final group game against France, a 78th-minute winner from Lars Elstrup gave Denmark an unlikely passage through to the semi-finals. Reaching the semi-finals was an incredible achievement in itself. Even without the talismanic Michael Laudrup, the side had achieved something very few would have believed prior to the tournament's start.

The semi-finals saw the Danes up against the Dutch. Holland were the reigning champions and featured the talents of Marco Van Basten, Frank Rijkaard and Ruud Gullit. After a 2-2 draw after extra time, the match went to penalties, when a Peter Schmeichel save from World Player of the Year Van Basten made the difference. Dennis Bergkamp, who had

---

218 Lars Eriksen, *Mike Gibbons and Rob Smyth, Danish Dynamite: The Story of Football's Greatest Cult Team* (London: Bloomsbury, 2014) pp.207-9

scored three in the tournament for Holland, believes that, although his side didn't underestimate the Danes, the victory over Germany in the group stage had meant they slowed down going into the semi-final, but 'little Denmark' had caused the Dutch to play one of their worst-ever games.[219] Denmark were in the final.

The newly unified Germany were their opponents in Gothenburg and would be a tough team to beat. The game itself wasn't a classic, and defensive Danish tactics certainly didn't help. However, goals from John Jensen and Kim Vilfort gave Denmark victory and with it the tournament. The game was also the last to use legal backpasses. Towards the end of the game, the Danish defence had utilised it to an incredible extent in order to waste time and stop the Germans from getting back into the game. Described by some as a 'rousing send-off' to the rule, most believed it to be the prime reason for the dullness of modern football.[220] It is a rule most believe the game is better off for removing.

For Michael Laudrup, hindsight has led to his regret over his premature international retirement. Indeed, soon after the victory, he returned to the international fold in time for the 1994 World Cup. Reaction around Europe centred on the 'underdog' story. The *Evening Herald* in Dublin ran the story with the headline 'Champions show gives heart to underdogs!'[221] Furthermore, the *Sunday Tribune* reported on the 'wild' celebrations that awaited the side on their return to Copenhagen. Despite a recorded 150,000 Danes in attendance, the article makes special note of the good behaviour of supporters, a feature which followed the fans throughout

---

219 Dennis Bergkamp, *Stillness and Speed: My Story* (London: Simon and Schuster, 2013) p.28

220 Adam Hurrey, 'Football was (re)invented in 1992: The early chaos of the backpass law', *ESPN* (9 August 2017) https://www.espn.co.uk/football/ english-premier-league/23/blog/post/3175840/premier-league-chaos-when-backpass-law-invented-in-1992

221 *Evening Herald*, 27 June 1992

the tournament. Following two decades of hooliganism and problems deep within the game, the Danish 'cooligans' had begun to reinvent the image of the sport.[222]

For a team as lowly ranked and thought of as Denmark to win a major international tournament, it gave underdogs around the world even more belief that they could do the impossible. This theme becomes even more relevant in the modern day, due to the staggering impact of money on the game. In recent years, the rise of super clubs has meant competition is often limited to a small number of teams. On the international stage, later triumphs for Greece in 2004 and to some extent Portugal in 2016 demonstrated that in football the whole is greater than the sum of its parts. What Denmark had, according to Vilfort, was togetherness and belief. 'We didn't have the best players, we had the best team.'[223]

222 *Sunday Tribune*, 28 June 1992

223 Kim Vilfort in Saj Chowdhury, 'Euro 1992: Denmark's Fairytale', *BBC Sport* (May 2012) https://www.bbc.co.uk/sport/football/17757335

35

The Premier League
and Champions League
are Born (1992)

As we have already seen, the introduction of technology to football and the fear it instilled in many clubs and supporters has been a running theme throughout the 50 moments. Indeed, such fears, like the initiation of radio and later television, did little to affect gate receipts. In 1992 these anxieties were to resurface as football was radically rebranded to suit an ever-changing world outside of the game. In England and abroad, two competitions would be changed forever. Their legacy to this day is still debated by millions of football fans around the world.

The Football League's top division in the early 1990s was beginning to undergo a resurgence on the world stage following England's 1990 World Cup performance. Furthermore, the ending of UEFA's five-year ban on English clubs in Europe had opened the nation to the European stage once again. Following the 1980s, which had been blighted by tragedy and hooliganism, the game was in need of a change of image. Football was attempting to shake off the image of 'a slum sport, played in slum stadiums, increasingly watched by slum people who deter decent folk from turning up'.[224]

---

224 *Sunday Times*, 19 May 1985

The Taylor Report would be vital in implementing change. The report made a number of recommendations about the infrastructure of the game. With hearts broken over Hillsborough, all-seater stadiums were implemented at the top level of football and CCTV cameras in grounds helped identify and root out the hooligan problem.[225] Indeed, even top-level attendances were rapidly dropping. In the 1991/92 season an average of just 21,723 was recorded. The start of the previous decade had seen this figure 25 per cent higher.[226]

Such low gates meant that by 1991 a high-court battle from the 'big five' clubs (Liverpool, Manchester United, Arsenal, Spurs and Everton) was won in order to negotiate their own television rights. By June, 16 clubs in the top flight had also declared their interest in creating a new division, separate from the Football League. Just three months later, the notion had the backing of all 22 teams. Clubs would therefore meet in order to discuss lucrative television deals, mainly with London Weekend Television. These meetings, often secretive, would shape the next quarter of a century of sport as ambition, money and influence took centre stage.[227] The FA Premier League was designed to bring in more money in order for English clubs to re-establish their dominance across the continent.

In terms of television, a bidding war was underway, with ITV, BBC and Sky all keen to secure the league for years to come. Ultimately, a £304 million bid from Sky was the winner. For the first time, the top level of English football would not be broadcast on terrestrial channels. Football fans would indeed need to pay to watch the 60 games which were

---

225 Gareth Thomas, 'The Birth of the Premier League: Did it Make or Break English Football?', *The Football History Boys* (17 January 2016)

226 Kevin Brandstatter and Paul Merkens, 'Attendances: England', *European Football Statistics* (2018) https://www.european-football-statistics.co.uk/attn/nav/attnengleague.htm

227 Joshua Robinson and Jonathan Clegg, *The Club: How the English Premier League Became the Wildest, Richest, Most Disruptive Force in Sports* (New York: Houghton Mifflin Harcourt, 2018) p.10

to be broadcast that season.[228] Furthermore, the kick-off times of these games would be different to the traditional 3pm start. For many, the traditions of the 'English' game were at risk of disappearing altogether.

The Premier League saw immediate success, not just from a financial viewpoint but in terms of attendances at grounds. Helped by the Taylor Report and the regular display of entertainment on television screens, supporters across the country once more flocked to their club's grounds to get a piece of the action. By the year 1999, attendances in the Premier League had risen to over 30,000 a game for the first time since 1973. Newly promoted clubs like Charlton Athletic would also profit, seeing a 49.4 per cent rise at the Valley.

The eradication of the back-pass rule and the gradual influx of foreign talent also helped to improve the game and its image on the continent. Klinnsman, Cantona, Gullit and Vialli were just some of the names who would provide opportunity for creativity and an openness to foreign tactics and ideas. The Premier League was to become the world's finest and most watched domestic league, arguably surpassing Serie A at the turn of the millennium. The surge in popularity and the success of reinvention is not to everyone's taste, however.

Around the same time, the UEFA European Cup went under a similar transformation. Once more, marketing was a key factor and television rights brought a new partnership between UEFA and TEAM Marketing AG. The new name was to be the UEFA Champions League and be battled by eight teams contesting two group stages following two knockout rounds. The winners of each group would meet in the final. Unlike the Premier League, the tournament would need longer to find a winning formula.

What the rebranding of the European Cup did was eventually create football's best club competition. Despite its

---

228 P. Millward, 'Domestic television rights and the birth of the Premier League', *The English Premier League: A Socio-Cultural Analysis* (London: Routledge, 2017)

first full season being tarnished by a match-fixing scandal involving winners Marseille, the following seasons saw good attendances and a ruthless dismantling of Cruyff's dream team by a resurgent AC Milan. The competition's format did prove a problem and has gone under significant changes in the last 25 years. Indeed, just 15 years ago there were two group stages before the knockout rounds. Fixture congestion led to UEFA remodelling the tournament into a format similar to the World Cup, with eight groups of four battling out a group stage before 16 teams fought to reach the final.

Recent seasons have shown a refined competition, safe in its own image. The 2018/19 edition has even been praised by some as 'the greatest tournament ever'.[229] The drama, particularly in the semi-finals where Liverpool and Tottenham made incredible comebacks at the expense of Barcelona and Ajax, has proven the Champions League to be alive and well as a new decade approaches.

The financial benefits and lucrative sponsorship deals open to those who enter has meant that even finishing fourth in one of Europe's top leagues now equates to as great an achievement as winning a domestic cup. In 2019/20 only Atalanta entered the tournament for the first time and 20 of the 32 sides remained the same as the season before. For some, this has led to the Champions League becoming a somewhat quasi-closed league, despite the notion that theoretically 'anyone can enter'.[230] Revenue redistribution has further propelled Europe's already successful teams like Juventus, Real Madrid, Barcelona, Liverpool, PSG and Man City into near invincible status. You can safely bet that one of these six sides will win the competition this season (2019/20).

---

229 Emlyn Begley, 'Champions League 2018-19: The Greatest Tournament Ever?', *BBC Sport* (2 June 2019) https://www.bbc.co.uk/sport/football/48354681

230 Wladimir Andreff, 'Sports events, economic impact and regulation', *Global Sport Marketing: Contemporary Issues and Practice* (London: Routledge, 2012) p.91

Similar arguments have been seen in England. Aside from the breath of fresh air which ran parallel to Leicester City's Premier League win in 2016 (Moment 48), the dominance of the division has been centred on a small number of teams. Since 2003, and the arrival of billionaire Roman Abramovich, only eight clubs have finished in the top four. Furthermore, the introduction of foreign players has split opinions. There is little doubt that the league has improved in terms of play and tactical innovation, but the decline of the English national team has been sourced by many to the lack of opportunity given to young academy prospects.

The influence of the Premier and Champions Leagues is of immense importance. Money rules the modern game and the reinvention of these competitions in 1992 has led the way for mass commercialisation and staggering wages. On the other hand, the influx of finances has also made for a better, safer game. The standard of football has no doubt improved massively as pitches and stadiums frequently undergo careful maintenance and the exposure of television has added to the prestige of the competitions they show. Today, we are often fed the narrative that football was a pure game before the invention of the Premier League, but this is simply not true. Football was in an increasingly precarious position in the late 1980s after decades of hooliganism, declining attendances and a laissez-faire attitude from the government. The Premier League will continue to split opinions for as long as it remains. One thing for certain is that in 2020 it is the greatest league on the planet and the Champions League is football's greatest competition. Who knows what they will do next?

1995–2004

36

The Bosman Ruling (1995)

Way back in 1907 (Moment 9) we saw how Billy Meredith helped form what would become the PFA. Two of the main things Meredith wanted to fight for was the abolition of the maximum wage that was imposed upon footballers, and greater freedom of moment for players who had been prevented by the power of their clubs. It would take until 1961 (Moment 21) for the maximum wage cap to be removed, but players were still prevented from leaving clubs on a free transfer at the end of their contracts. This meant a club could keep unhappy (but potentially valuable) players on their books until a club paid them an agreed transfer fee; as Sir Alex Ferguson puts it, players were 'partially imprisoned'.[231]

Jean-Marc Bosman, however, changed the footballing world in the 1990s. Bosman, a Belgian midfielder, was coming to the end of his time with his side RFC Liège, whom he had joined for roughly £66,000 in 1990. His two-year spell with the club was not a particularly positive one and so Bosman was looking to move on at the end of his deal. French second-tier side Dunkirk had offered him a deal he wanted to sign, but Bosman was prevented from leaving the club on a free transfer because RFC Liège were holding out for a fee of

---

231 Alex Ferguson and Michael Moritz, *Leading* (London: Hodder & Stoughton, 2015) p.311

roughly four times the size of what they had paid.[232] The deal fell through, with Dunkirk failing to agree to pay the inflated fee demanded, and Liège cut Bosman's wages by 75 per cent, freezing him out of the first team whilst retaining his registration.[233] Bosman later remarked, 'They thought that I had become four times better if I wanted to leave and four times worse if I wanted to sign again for them.'[234] The bitter dispute would lead to perhaps the most significant legal battle in the history of the beautiful game.

Bosman's legal fight took five years to complete, the tussle going to the European Court of Justice (ECJ). The argument of Bosman and his lawyers was based upon the EU's Treaty of Rome (1957), which guaranteed freedom of movement for players anywhere in the European Economic Community. The legal wrangling ruined Bosman's career – he was banned from the Belgian league by the country's association. Other clubs would not sign the perceived troublemaker, Bosman only featuring for second-tier French sides Saint-Quentin and Saint-Denis for short periods. In 1995 the ECJ made their ruling, finding in favour of Bosman and setting a precedent that would change football forever. Footballers could now move on a 'free transfer' at the end of their contracts providing they were over the age of 24. Under that age, clubs would receive a fee but should that not be agreed a tribunal would dictate the fee instead.[235] The power had firmly swung to the players and has remained that way ever since.

Newspapers in the months leading to the judgement were very cautious, fearing that any shift in the transfer regulations would give 'top players colossal power and wealth, while putting

---

232 *The Independent*, 21 September 1995

233 Matt Slater, 'Bosman ruling: 20 years on since ex-RFC Liege player's victory', *BBC* (15 December 2015) https://www.bbc.co.uk/sport/football/35097223

234 *The Guardian*, 12 December 2015

235 *Liverpool Echo*, 15 December 1995

lower league clubs at risk'.[236] When the ECJ delivered their verdict, the papers were in no doubt of the size of the decision, the *Liverpool Echo* reporting that a 'player who figures in the comparative backwater of the Belgian fourth division, could today go down in history as the man who changed the face of football'.[237] The prediction was not wrong as Edgar Davids became the first world-class player to benefit from Bosman, moving from Ajax to Milan in 1996. Since then, it has enabled hundreds of moves, including Steve McManaman (Liverpool to Real Madrid) in 1999, Sol Campbell (Tottenham to Arsenal) in 2001, Robert Lewandowski (Borussia Dortmund to Real Madrid) in 2014 and Aaron Ramsey (Arsenal to Juventus) in 2019.

The impact of the Bosman Law saw the rise of the football agent. Players could demand massive signing-on fees as their new clubs were saving money because of the free transfer. Of course, whilst it freed all clubs to benefit, as every football club in the world has, it has been infamously ranted about by managers. Sir Alex Ferguson commented that, 'Once the European Court of Justice ruled that clubs no longer had to pay transfer fees after the expiration of a player's contract, all hell broke loose. Suddenly it was a free-for-all.'[238] Then-Blackpool manager Ian Holloway also exploded about Bosman in a press conference in 2010, after Manchester United and Wayne Rooney fell out over an improved contract and the prospect of a free transfer loomed.

However, while Bosman can be seen as a transformative moment, those reflecting upon football's transfer market also play down its impact. Borja Garcia writes that 'Bosman was not the starting point of what has been labelled by some as modern football'. He likens it to 'an accelerator', pointing to the fact that football had been in the process of changing over

---

236 *Irish Independent*, 23 September 1995

237 *Liverpool Echo*, 15 December 1995

238 Alex Ferguson and Michael Moritz, *Leading* (London: Hodder & Stoughton, 2015), p.311

the 1990s across Europe as it was. Garcia notes that people had become 'hostile' towards UEFA and this was joined by clubs and leagues who wanted a bigger share of the profits to be made in European football.[239] So Bosman, whether as transformative as remembered or not, is still controversial to this day – a top 50 moment? Absolutely! .

---

239 Borja Garcia, in Duval, Antoine and Van Rompuy, Ben (eds.) *The Legacy of Bosman: Revisiting the Relationship Between EU Law and Sport* (The Hague: T.M.C. ASSER Press, 2016) pp.28-9

37

FIFA World Cup 1998 – Owen, Ronaldo and France (1998)

The World Cup in 1998 is remembered for so many reasons: France winning on home soil, David Beckham's red card, Michael Owen's stunning goal, Davor Šuker and, of course, Brazilian Ronaldo. This World Cup would be the largest ever – 32 teams instead of the 24 previously making the finals. France, the host nation, were hunting their first-ever title, whilst Brazil, the current holders, were well fancied for another success – 1998 would be a special tournament.

The group stages passed by without too much incident: France won all three of their games, Brazil won two whilst also losing surprisingly to Norway, Germany and England also progressed safely, along with Argentina and Croatia too. Scotland's competition, meanwhile, was cut short after their three group games. A draw secured by a Craig Burley goal against Norway ensured the Scots would not go home pointless, despite losses in their other matches. Group D would see the biggest upsets, top seeds Spain failing to qualify for the knockout rounds and Bulgaria (who were excellent in 1994) finishing bottom of the group.

An all-South American last-16 tie between Brazil and Chile beckoned, Brazil's Ronaldo, Rivaldo and Bebeto having made flying starts to the tournament. This continued versus

Chile as Ronaldo netted twice alongside two more from César Sampaio in a 4-1 victory – safe passage to the quarter-finals. France, meanwhile, needed extra time and a Laurent Blanc goal to see off Paraguay in Lens and continue their dream of a home World Cup victory.

The most famous clash of the first knockout round was undoubtedly Argentina v England. On 30 June, the rivals of 1986 (Moment 30) would meet again on the world stage. The match got off to a rip-roaring start as Gabriel Batistuta scored a penalty in the fifth minute, whilst Shearer responded with a penalty of his own four minutes later. Then came one of the moments of the World Cup – Michael Owen, the 18-year-old Liverpool striker, scored a goal to announce himself to the globe. The BBC's John Motson later described it as 'a Maradona moment',[240] Owen picking the ball up on the halfway line before speeding towards goal, beating two defenders as he did so. His powerful finish gave England the lead and justified manager Glenn Hoddle's comparison to Ronaldo before the tournament, who likened his 'electrifying pace' and eye for goal to that of the Brazilian.[241]

The stunning solo goal had put England 2-1 up, but on the stroke of half-time Inter Milan's Javier Zanetti levelled the match. The biggest turning point came just two minutes into the second half, Manchester United midfielder David Beckham kicking out at Diego Simeone right under the referee's nose – Beckham was dismissed and faced a 'gauntlet of hate' back home.[242] The English managed to take the game into extra time, but Argentina failed to find a way through. Penalties would be needed to settle this fixture. Hernan Crespo and Paul Ince both missed their side's second penalty and, with everyone else scoring, it came down to the fifth and final spot-kick. Step up David Batty ...

240 *The Telegraph*, 25 May 2018
241 *Liverpool Echo*, 1 July 1998
242 *Dublin Evening Herald*, 15 July 1998

the Yorkshireman missed and England were out, penalty heartbreak yet again!

In the quarter-finals, hosts France would see the return of Juventus midfielder Zinedine Zidane to the side, following his suspension after a red card versus Saudi Arabia in the groups. The hosts would need penalties at the Stade de France to put away the Italians after a 0-0 draw; the Croatians (who dominated Germany 3-0) would await in the semis. Argentina lost to the Dutch whilst Brazil were given a scare by Denmark. They snuck through 3-2, with Rivaldo the hero of that game as he secured a brace to add to Bebeto's early opener.

The semi-finals of a so far gripping tournament would see Brazil face the Netherlands and France play Croatia. Ronaldo, who had come off the back of a 34-goal debut season at Inter Milan, scored just after the half-time break and seemingly put the favourites into another final. However, Patrick Kluivert (of city rivals AC Milan) had other ideas and just three minutes from time secured another half an hour of bonus football for the fans watching at home! Another penalty shoot-out would be needed to find a winner and it would be misses from Phillip Cocu and Ronald de Boer that helped secure the 4-2 victory for the defending champions Brazil, sending them to a Stade de France final on 12 July 1998.

Croatia, who had enjoyed a superb tournament in France, were facing the hosts in front of over 76,000 fans. An unlikely hero emerged for the French in Saint-Denis, as right-back Lilian Thuram scored twice in the second half for his country. With Croatia's Golden Boot winner Davor Šuker (six goals) having given the underdogs the lead just after the break, a quick response from Thuram helped level the scores. The Parma defender then netted in the 70th minute to give France a 2-1 victory and give them a shot at a first World Cup title.

So the stage for the final – hosts France versus favourites to defend their title Brazil, mouth-watering! However, to everyone's surprise, Ronaldo (who had been the star of the tournament) was left off the team sheet when the names were published on the day of the final. It was later revealed that Roberto Carlos, who shared a room with Ronaldo, had found his team-mate suffering a convulsion that led to the striker being rushed to hospital.[243] The Brazil squad were shocked and distressed by what some of them had witnessed in the build-up to the evening's game, but suddenly, just before kick-off, Ronaldo was reinstated into the side. What was going on? It turned out medical exams passed him fit to play, but the match that took place would prove otherwise.

Les Bleus opened the scoring via a Zidane header 27 minutes into the final. Brazil struggled to create chances and, when they did, they weren't taken. This was compounded by a second Zidane header in first-half injury time, giving the French an unassailable lead. Brazil spurned more chances to get back into the tie in the second 45 minutes, before Emmanuel Petit rounded off the scoring in the 93rd minute. France had their first-ever World Cup triumph and 'Merci, Zizou!' was projected on to the Champs-Élysées that night in celebration of their star man.[244]

For Brazil, the loss would be as devastating as *Maracanazo* in 1950 (Moment 16). There would be no fifth world title and the inquest began about the decision to start Ronaldo after his health scare. Some blamed Nike, sponsors of the Brazilian team, for influencing the inclusion of the talisman – something the sportswear company strongly denied.[245] This did not convince some newspapers though, as the *Reading Evening Post* drew their own conclusions that cited 'commercial pressures on Ronaldo and the Brazilian team forced the youngster to play, effectively destroying Brazil's chances of victory'.[246] For the South Americans, 1998 would

---

243 Clemente A. Lisi, *A History of the World Cup* (Plymouth: Scarecrow, 2011) pp.288-9

244 Thomas Dunmore and Scott Murray, *Soccer for Dummies* (Indianapolis: John Wiley & Sons INC., 2013) p. 313

245 Clemente A. Lisi, *A History of the World Cup*, pp.288-9

246 *Reading Evening Post*, 17 July 1998

always remain a question of 'what if?', but for France it was *the* joyous moment the football-loving nation had long been dreaming of.

38

Manchester United's Treble-Winning Season (1998/99)

The 1998/99 season is the most successful in the long and great history of Manchester United Football Club. With Sir Alex Ferguson at the helm, United had won four titles in the Premier League era, the league and FA Cup double coming in 1994 and 1996.

They had become a formidable force, despite *Match of the Day* pundit Alan Hansen declaring in August 1995: 'You can't win anything with kids.' Those 'kids' were the famous 'Class of 1992', featuring David Beckham, the Neville brothers, Paul Scholes, Ryan Giggs and Nicky Butt. It would be 1998/99 that would become their crowning glory.

Over the summer of 1998, some old faces left Old Trafford, Brian McClair and Gary Pallister the notable men to move on. Fergie's young but impressive side would be supplemented by the arrivals of defender Jaap Stam, winger Jesper Blomqvist and striker Dwight Yorke. However, things got off to a difficult start in August, with United losing the Charity Shield 3-0 to rivals Arsenal. That loss, though, would be one of just five throughout the course of the coming season – only three occurring in the Premier League. United would also have a spell of 33 games unbeaten in all competitions starting on Boxing Day 1998.

So to the Premier League title and from gameweek one Man United had to show that 'never say die' attitude akin to a Sir Alex side. Trailing 2-0 in the 79th minute, a Teddy Sheringham strike would bring the Red Devils back into it. Then the man who would become Mr Reliable, David Beckham, netted to level the game in injury time. This result would help keep an unbeaten home record till December when Middlesbrough would record a surprising 3-2 victory. This, though, would be the only time United would lose at Old Trafford all season. Arsenal would push the title race all the way till the end of the campaign, but Man United secured the title with 79 points, one clear of their rivals. One trophy wrapped up!

The FA Cup, meanwhile, was not an easy cup to secure. Seeing off Merseyside enemies Liverpool 2-1 in the fourth round, Chelsea then took them to a replay in the quarter-finals. Drawing 0-0 at home, a Yorke double put United into a semi-final clash with Arsenal. The two sides met at neutral Villa Park, but a 0-0 draw meant they'd have to do it all again in a replay just four days later. With Beckham on the scoresheet the game would finish 1-1 and head to extra time. Ryan Giggs netted a 109th-minute winner, leading to that famous, topless, hairy-chested celebration.

In the final at Wembley, the Red Devils would meet Newcastle United with the former Man United target Alan Shearer hoping to lift his first FA Cup for his home-town club. Things were seemingly disrupted, too, by an injury to captain Roy Keane inside ten minutes. However, his replacement, Sheringham, played a 'delightful' one-two with Scholes before slotting home to make it 1-0 just two minutes after coming on.[247] Scholes then netted the other side of half-time to help United lift the FA Cup. Even if they lost in the Champions League Final just four days later, the Red

247 BBC, 'Double joy for Man United', *BBC Sport* (22 May 1999) http://news.bbc.co.uk/1/hi/sport/football/fa_cup/350192.stm

Devils would still have a league and cup double, their third of the 1990s.

To the final piece of that treble jigsaw. Manchester United were attempting to become the first ever English club to win a treble. United's group contained Bayern Munich, Barcelona and Brøndby and, despite drawing four of their six games (both times 3-3 thrillers with Barça), the 6-2 and 5-0 wins over Danish side Brøndby were enough to take second place in their group. Keane was clear about the club's intentions – to lift the Champions League: 'You want to be winning trophies, especially the European Cup. We're now capable of going on to win it.'[248]

United would then go through the knockout rounds unbeaten, with Italian sides Inter Milan and Juventus put to the sword. Bayern Munich would await on 26 May 1999 – it would become one of the greatest finishes to a final ever. Mario Basler gave the Germans a 1-0 lead after just six minutes and had seemingly stolen the treble from Sir Alex's men. Then the unthinkable happened. Sheringham netted in the 91st minute to seemingly salvage extra time, before Ole Gunnar Solskjær sent himself down in United history. A 93rd-minute goal won the match and sent the red half of Manchester into delirium – United were treble winners in spectacular style!

Following 'one of the most remarkable escape acts in soccer history',[249] United arrived back in Manchester to a heroes' welcome – over 350,000 fans greeting the team as calls were made for Alex Ferguson to be knighted.[250] That call was answered in the Queen's Birthday Honours that summer, Sir Alex rewarded for his services to the beautiful game. Sir Alex would continue his dominance of the English game till his retirement in 2013. He won 13 Premier League titles with

---

248 Mark Froggatt, '#Treble99: Qualifying From the Group of Death', *Manchester United* (9 December 2018) https://www.manutd.com/en/news/detail/treble-99-united-1-bayern-munich-1-on-9-december-1998.

249 *Irish Independent*, 27 May 1999

250 *Aberdeen Press and Journal*, 28 May 1999

the Red Devils, five FA Cups, four League Cups, ten FA Community Shields and two UEFA Champions League trophies. 1999's treble, though, would be his finest hour.

The first international between England and Scotland saw a clash of culture and playing styles. It was the start of the game's oldest rivalry

DRIBBLING·

The Ibrox Disaster brought into question the safety and standards of football stadia. Sadly, it wouldn't be the game's last major tragedy

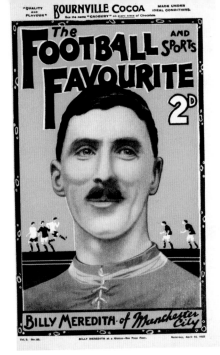

Billy Meredith was in some ways the first true footballing celebrity. His influence went beyond the pitch and deep into an ever-changing society

Over 250,000 people are estimated to have arrived at Wembley for the 1923 FA Cup Final

An unfamiliar trophy lift. FIFA president Jules Rimet presents the World Cup to Dr Paul Jude, president of the Uruguayan Football Association

Seventy years on, thousands of Torino supporters still visit the site of the Superga disaster each year

German forward Max Morlock pulls a goal back in his country's remarkable comeback against favourites Hungary

England captain Bobby Moore holds aloft the World Cup to a jubilant Wembley Stadium

The El Salvador side that beat rivals Honduras in Mexico City. Victory would lead to war in the days that followed

Emlyn Hughes lifts the European Cup to the thousands of travelling reds in Rome

Controversial genius Diego Maradona celebrates victory over England after his infamous display in Mexico City

Alongside continuing calls for justice, the Kop remembers the 96 Liverpool supporters who died at Hillsborough

Despite having not qualified, Denmark players celebrate one of the biggest shocks in football history

World Player of the Year Ronaldo looks down dejected as his World Cup comes to a sorry and mysterious end in Paris

Zidane walks past the World Cup following his late dismissal for a headbutt on Italian Marco Materazzi

Tiki-taka master Pep Guardiola embraces Lionel Messi after victory in the Copa Del Rey

A carnival atmosphere awaited players and fans from across the world as South Africa put on a show to remember

Sergio Aguero writes his name in Premier League history after his last-gasp winner seals the title for Manchester City

Germany celebrate as Brazilian players slump to the ground following a humilating defeat in Belo Horizonte

Referee Felix Zwayer checks his pitchside monitor during a Champions League fixture in Salzburg

39

'I am a Special One' –
José Mourinho (2004)

Two 2004 moments were considered for this spot, with Greece winning the European Championships in as stunning and unexpected a style as Denmark doing the same in 1992 (Moment 34). However, we could not miss out this man. Hate him or love him, José Mourinho is someone who has dominated the headlines of the football world for the last 15 years. 2004 was the moment he arrived on the scene, announcing to the world 'I think I am a special one' upon being appointed Chelsea boss.[251] He asked for us not to think of him as arrogant; well I'm not sure that happened ... but he has gone about proving himself ever since!

José Mourinho, known by Barcelona fans derogatorily as 'The translator' because of his role there as Bobby Robson's translator, first shot to real fame at FC Porto. He won back-to-back leagues in 2003 and 2004 and then stunned Europe with an amazing Champions League victory in 2004. Having put out Chelsea in the semi-finals, Porto put Monaco away 3-0 in the final. This attracted the attention of ambitious new Chelsea owner Roman Abramovich, who appointed him as

---

251 BBC, 'Chelsea appoint Mourinho', *BBC Sport* (2 June 2004) http://news.bbc.co.uk/sport1/hi/football/teams/c/chelsea/3765263.stm.

manager in the summer of 2004. Mourinho ruffled feathers instantly: 'We have top players and, sorry if I'm arrogant, but we now have a top manager.'[252] I think it's safe to say that if you weren't a Chelsea fan you disliked José!

For all his ego, coupled with the finances of Abramovich José's Chelsea won the Premier League in his very first season, along with a League Cup. The next season? He won the league again! Mourinho's men were well-organised and incredibly difficult to beat, even Sir Alex Ferguson acknowledging, 'I didn't win a game at Stamford Bridge after Mourinho arrived.'[253] Despite setting an unbeaten home record by the start of the 2007/08 campaign, over 64 consecutive games, 'The Special One' and Abramovich fell out. In September 2007 Mourinho 'astonishingly' left the club to the devastation of many Chelsea supporters.[254]

After the rest of the season off, Inter Milan became the new venue for José. In Italy the Serie A title was secured within his first season yet again. And yet again this was retained in 2009/10 in José's spectacular treble-winning season – Serie A, Coppa Italia and the UEFA Champions League trophy (2-0 vs Bayern Munich). Following this stunning season, Real Madrid came knocking and José took the chance to move to Spain with *Los Blancos*.

Real Madrid was where Mourinho's rivalry with then Barcelona boss Pep Guardiola was ignited. The two did battle for the La Liga title over Jose's three years at the Santiago Bernabéu, José winning the title once, adding to one Copa del Rey and one Supercopa de España. Whilst popular again with the fans of the club he manages, José doesn't always win fans at other clubs. His defensively focussed style, which prioritises winning over beautiful football, is undoubtedly successful but not always enjoyable, Mourinho accused of 'parking the bus'

252 *Ibid*

253 Alex Ferguson, *My Autobiography* (London: Hodder and Stoughton, 2013) p.164

254 *The Guardian*, 20 September 2007

wherever he has gone. This did not stop Chelsea bringing Jose back in 2013, however, Mourinho again delivering a Premier League title (2014/15) and a League Cup. José's relationship with Abramovich had seemingly never fully recovered, and a poor start to the 2015/16 campaign and a 'palpable discord with the players' saw Mourinho leaving Chelsea for a second time in December 2015.[255]

Following Sir Alex Ferguson's retirement at Manchester United, success was not quickly forthcoming for the Red Devils. In May 2016 Mourinho took the reins at Old Trafford, securing the FA Community Shield within weeks before winning the Europa League the following May. The pressure was on Mourinho to succeed again and challenge his old adversary Pep Guardiola, who was by now at Manchester City. In 2017/18 Mourinho was criticised for United's last-16 Champions League exit to Sevilla,[256] but in the league a second-place finish was recorded. This was seemingly far beyond the capabilities of the squad at Old Trafford, who in subsequent seasons struggled to break into the magic 'top four'. In December 2018, with just seven wins in the first 17 Premier League matches of the new campaign, Mourinho's time in the north-west was brought to a close.

Mourinho took a break from football after United, spending time offering his wisdom to TV channels across the world. His expertise was loved and admired by viewers, but it was clear Mou was not ready to put away his coaching manuals yet. In November 2019 he was announced as a surprise replacement at another London club, Tottenham Hotspur. Mourinho would bring a very different style to outgoing manager Mauricio Pochettino, but the (almost) guaranteed success he brings was enough to tempt Spurs to pursue the Portuguese legend.

José Mourinho's career has spanned four countries, managing five of the biggest clubs in the history of football.

---

255 *The Guardian*, 17 December 2015

256 *Daily Express*, 14 March 2018

He has won trophies wherever he has gone, his managerial trophy cabinet reading: 2x Primeira Liga (POR), 1x Taça de Portugal (POR), 1x Supertaça Cândido de Oliveira (POR), 2x UEFA Champions League, 2x UEFA Cup/Europa League, 3x Premier League (ENG), 1x FA Cup (ENG), 4x Football League Cup (ENG), 2x FA Community Shield (ENG), 2x Serie A (ITA), 1x Coppa Italia (ITA), 1x Supercoppa Italiana (ITA), 1x La Liga (ESP), 1x Copa del Rey (ESP) and 1x Supercopa de España (ESP).[257] Not bad for a translator eh? Special? I think so!

---

257 Mourinho's managerial record as of January 2020

40

The Miracle of Istanbul (2005)

'Six minutes. Think about it for a moment. What exactly can you do in six minutes?'[258]

In 2004 Spanish manager Rafael Benitez joined the Reds. In front of him was, to quote Steven Gerrard, 'a squad which needed strengthening and improving'.[259] Benitez's job was huge, but with the acquisitions of Xabi Alonso and Luis Garcia, and the undeniable home-grown talents of Steven Gerrard and Jamie Carragher, he at least could boast a strong spine. Following a nail-biting Champions League group campaign, which saw the Reds minutes away from a group-stage exit, the first knockout round would see them face Bayer Leverkusen. Victories both home and away set up an emotional tie against Juventus (see Moment 29). In May, a Luis Garcia 'ghost goal' saw off new, yet bitter rivals Chelsea. Milan had fewer problems and comfortably made it to the Ataturk Stadium in Istanbul. The match itself saw Milan as clear favourites.

Fifty-six seconds. Maldini. Milan 1-0 Liverpool.

Not the desired start for Benitez's men. The XI selected to start the match had been a surprise from the off as his usual pragmatic approach was left, in favour of a more attacking style.

---

258 John Williams, *The Miracle of Istanbul: Liverpool FC, From Paisley to Benitez* (London: Mainstream, 2005) p.1

259 Steven Gerrard, *My Autobiography* (London: Bantam 2006) p.298

Before long, Milan were tearing Liverpool to shreds. Brazilian playmaker Kaka was running the show and two quick-fire Hernan Crespo goals gave the Italians an unassailable lead. At half-time it was Milan 3-0 Liverpool.

'As I walked towards the dressing room, I was suffering from a depressing combination of despondency and humiliation. I couldn't bear to lift my head up and glimpse at the faces in the crowd.'[260]

The second half was changed in a mere six minutes. Following the introduction of German midfielder Didi Hamann, the Liverpool system changed. Suddenly, the flair of Kaka was stifled and the rampaging full-backs of Milan were forced to defend. In the 54th minute, captain Steven Gerrard headed Liverpool back into the game. His celebration was to rouse the euphoric support into a cacophony of noise. Within two minutes, forgotten man Vladimir Smicer had smashed in from 20 yards, and four minutes after that Gerrard was brought down by Gattuso for a penalty. Alonso's spot-kick was saved by Dida, before he thumped the rebound into the roof of the net. Milan 3-3 Liverpool.

'I could not believe it. It seemed impossible ... I think this is part of the beauty of football. That match is part of destiny, of things that can't be explained. Even today I can't believe it.'[261]

Into extra time. Extra time saw Milan come back at Liverpool. Applying intense pressure to increasingly fatigued legs was sure to pay off. In the 117th minute, just three minutes before the end of play, one of the greatest double-saves in football history was made. Firstly, a downward header from Shevchenko was denied by Jerzy Dudek before a point-blank reaction deflected a certain goal over the crossbar. For

---

260 Jamie Carragher, *Carra: My Autobiography* (London: Bantam Press, 2008) p.326

261 Hernan Crespo in an interview with *The Guardian* in 2015 – ten years after the final in Istanbul https://www.theguardian.com/football/2015/may/25/hernan-crespo-milan-liverpool-istanbul

Shevchenko, it was now he knew the cup was destined for Liverpool. In the resulting shoot-out, Serginho, Pirlo and 'Sheva' himself missed, meaning the cup was returning to Merseyside.

'I will never watch that match again', are the words from Andrea Pirlo's autobiography which perhaps summarise best the feeling amongst the Milan players. The club were left to pick up the pieces of defeat and indeed would gain revenge two years later against Liverpool in 2007. The feeling of victory in Athens offered some relief, but the scars of Istanbul still leave painful memories to this day. The Milan midfielder would go as far as saying that the defeat in 2005 should be placed in the centre of all *Rossoneri* achievements as a message to future generations that 'feeling invincible is the first step on the path to the point of no return'.[262] The Liverpool side, on the other hand, became legendary figures, not just amongst their own supporters but across the football world. The impossible had happened.

So what did this mean for football? Firstly, victory would bring the Premier League to the forefront of European football as the division became the continent's best and most competitive. Furthermore, from the following season, 2005/06, to 2008/09, English clubs filled ten out of the 16 Champions League semi-finalist places. Perhaps most importantly though, it once again helped us to take note of the underdog. It showed that team spirit, passionate supporters and resilience can go a long way. It gave fuel to the notion that every minute in a football match is as important as the next. As well as giving spirit to the underdog, it also meant winning sides would not take their victory for granted. A game is never over. In just six unpredictable minutes, you can go from forlorn despondency to the centre of the universe.

---

262 Andrea Pirlo, *I Think Therefore I Play* (London: Backpage Press, 2014)

2006-2010

41. Zidane (2006)

42. *Calciopoli* Scandal (2006)

43. David Beckham Joins LA Galaxy (2007)

44. Tiki-Taka (2008)

45. The World Cup Arrives in
Africa (2010)

41

Zidane (2006)

What word comes to your mind when we mention the name Zinedine Zidane? The answer is almost certainly head-butt. It is a somewhat acrimonious response following what was an unbelievable career. Today, we know him as the manager – a leader who led Real Madrid to three successive Champions League victories, an unbelievable achievement in itself. Nevertheless, the end of his playing career in 2006 was to be tarnished by an incident at the end of France's unfancied, yet impressive, run to the World Cup Final in Germany. Of course, the French captain's misconduct was not unique to major finals. What made it so instantaneously infamous was that *Zidane* had done it. A player so revered, idolised and so well-respected.

A centre-midfielder at 6ft 2in, the way he moved about the pitch was more akin to a gazelle. Combined with flair, skill and physicality, he was in some ways the perfect footballer. In France '98 he had played a pivotal role in Les Bleus' home triumph. Zidane scored twice in the final to sink Brazil's *Selecao*. This instantly propelled the Algerian-born star to world-class status and his name was renowned around the world. Three years later, after a successful spell in Italy with Juventus, he would become a *Galactico* at Real Madrid. His left-foot volley in the 2002 Champions League Final was the epitome of the man – sheer class.

Prior to the 2006 World Cup, Zidane announced his retirement from the game, which was to follow the end of the tournament. The news came as a shock for many, with the influential midfielder only 33 years old. Having previously retired from international duty in 2004, he had been convinced to re-join the national team for the World Cup. Zidane saw his poor club form as the main reason for his decision. 'This is definitive. I'm stopping everything.'[263] The firmness in his stance brought the football world together in reflection of his incredible career; maybe there was to be one final chapter to cement his staggering legacy.

Going into the campaign, France were not thought of as favourites. Their aging squad still featured a handful of players from the triumph in 1998. Zidane, Barthez, Thuram and Wiltord were just four of seven over the age of 30. Only Frank Ribery was younger than 24. Brazil, Italy, England and Portugal were considered a level ahead of their French rivals. With squads full of world-class talent and attacking flair, they would seemingly have too much for Zidane's side.

Fortunately for the French, a comfortable group stage would follow. Determined not to underestimate their opposition as they had in 2002, the team managed by Raymond Domenech would play a brand of conservative football. Strong at the back and quick on the break, they would qualify behind neighbours Switzerland. As runners-up in Group H, the French would face a daunting run to Berlin. First, a youthful Spanish side were beaten in Hanover, before a meeting with Brazil in Frankfurt. The fixture would be a repeat of the 1998 World Cup Final, a game where Zidane had first propelled himself to fame across the footballing world after his two headed goals sealed a home victory for Les Bleus.

A Thierry Henry goal 12 minutes after half-time would send unfancied France into the World Cup semi-finals.

---

263 Zinedine Zidane in Alex Livie, 'Zidane announces retirement', *Sky Sports* (May 2006) https://www.skysports.com/football/news/11835/2374656/zidane-announces-retirement

Beating a Brazilian side, featuring the likes of Ronaldinho, Ronaldo and Roberto Carlos, would need something truly special. In Zidane, that was what they found. Described by some as a 'second coming', the performance from Zizou was more akin to an act of divine intervention. *The Guardian* was particularly impressed with his display, likening it to a 'phoenix rising from the ashes'. Playing with such majesty, they were sure his performance would be 'seared in the memories of those present'.[264]

'Over the past ten years, there's been no one like him, he has been the best player in the world.'[265]

Pelé was right, there was no one like Zidane. France, now seemingly playing with the world behind them, beat Portugal in the semi-finals and set up a mouth-watering clash against three-time winners Italy. In Berlin, the stage was set – two great teams with world-class players battling it out to be the best in the world. Step forward Zinedine Zidane. After just seven minutes he gave France the lead from the penalty spot. What truly summed up the man was the way in which he did it – a cheeky Panenka off the crossbar.

Marco Materazzi equalised for Italy and after an exhilarating, end-to-end contest, the match went to extra time. In the additional 30 minutes, a true moment of madness happened. Following a tirade of insults from Materazzi aimed at Zidane in the 110th minute, the Frenchman turned around and planted a head-butt square on the chest of his Italian counterpart. The millions watching around the world were stunned. In Zidane's last-ever game he had been sent off. As he walked off unapologetically, he passed the World Cup trophy. There remains something truly poignant about the image.

Zidane's indiscretion drew a mixed reaction from around the world. In France, although many sympathised with their messiah, some felt him responsible for the eventual defeat.

264 *The Guardian*, 2 July 2006
265 *The Independent*, 2 July 2006

Frank Leboeuf said he was 'ashamed' of the reaction from Zidane and saw it as the prime reason for the Italian victory.[266] The watching audience overwhelmingly took the side of Zizou, some even wishing he had head-butted Materazzi harder![267] The phrase 'flawed genius' was found in a number of articles as the mercurial number ten retired. A career, often seen as a work of art, blighted by 14 red cards.

---

266 Frank Leboeuf on *BBC Radio Five Live*, July 2006
267 Simon Critchley, *What We Think About When We Think About Football* (London: Profile, 2017) p.117

42

Calciopoli Scandal (2006)

Despite Italy basking in the glory of becoming world champions for the fourth time in July, an emerging scandal was looming over the heads of many of those who played in the nation's great triumph. The beautiful game, as we have seen, has never been too far from corruption and scandal. From Billy Meredith's bribery scandal in 1906 to Marseille's disputed Champions League win in 1993, such levels of dishonesty have tarnished the game. Of course, it is not just football that has seen this kind of disruptive influence. Indeed, the 'bloodgate' episode in rugby and the wealth of drug cheats in cycling throughout the 1990s mean that for many the drive to win has clouded their reasons for playing in the first place.

In 2005 Italian football held a firm place amongst the best in the world. Its domestic league, Serie A, had boomed in the 1990s and during the early 2000s was still producing Champions League winners and finalists. The starting XIs of teams like Milan and Juventus were testament to the success. A mix of home-grown talent with the very best the world had to offer, Serie A seemed destined to stay at the summit of European football for the foreseeable future. But all was not as it seemed; Italian football was in fact slowly dying.[268] The

---

268 Adam Digby, *Juventus: A History in Black and White* (Huddersfield: Ockley, 2015)

rise of the Premier League and La Liga meant superstars were increasingly being turned by the lucrative nature of England and Spain.

Both the 2004/05 and 2005/06 *Scudettos* had been won by Juventus. Building on a Champions League Final appearance in 2003, the Turin club had dominated domestic competition. Despite playing a brand of football which failed to set the world alight, it was functional and gathered points at an incredible rate. At the centre of the success was Luciano Moggi, the chief managing director. Moggi had been in charge of securing new players for the club, and with the likes of Zlatan Ibrahimovic joining in 2004 he seemed to be building a team which could compete not just in Italy, but in Europe.

The *Calciopoli* (Footballgate) Scandal was initially uncovered in May 2006. Just weeks before the start of the World Cup, what made this moment stand out was the sheer scale of the corruption. Incredibly, alongside Serie A champions Juventus were some of the biggest clubs in Italy. Milan, Fiorentina, Lazio and Reggina were also brought into question. This 'distinctive characteristic' is what sets it apart from previous cases of match-fixing.[269] The concerns were centred on a match-fixing network that spanned the previous two seasons. Telephone conversations were recorded as high-ranking officials at the named football clubs and the refereeing union collaborated to appoint favourable referees to make favourable decisions for sums of money.

Moggi was central to the corruption. The scandal has even been called 'Moggiopoli' by many commentators due to his incredible influence over the events that followed. The director claimed that he had only asked for favourable referees to put the *Bianconeri* on a level playing field. For Moggi, other clubs were fixing games earlier than Juventus and so this was the only way to make things fair. His influence on matches went

---

269 Alessandro Baroncelli, 'Calciopoli: Reasons and Scenarios for the Soccer Scandal', *Italian Politics: The Centre-Left's Poisoned Victory* (New York: Berghahn, 2007) p.226

as high up as UEFA officials and even Italian government ministers.

Calciopoli rocked European football and very nearly tore the Italian game apart. The punishments, long debated and argued legally, would eventually see Milan deducted 30 points for the 2005/06 Serie A season and eight points for 2006/07. Fiorentina, meanwhile, were thrown out of the 2006/07 Champions League and deducted 15 points for 2006/07, Lazio were thrown out of the 2006/07 UEFA Cup and deducted three points in 2006/07, and Reggina were fined €100,000 and deducted 11 points in 2006/07. Juventus received the heaviest punishments of all the sides. Juventus were stripped of the 2004/05 Serie A title (which remains unassigned), whilst Inter Milan were given the 2005/06 championship. Juve were relegated from the top flight to Serie B and deducted nine points for the 2006/07 campaign.

Many believed Juventus would struggle to retain players, having some of the best footballers in Europe who would easily walk into other top sides. However, in the scandal that stretched back to 2004, players insisted they were totally unaware of any match fixing. Whilst star striker Zlatan Ibrahimović and defenders Lilian Thuram and Fabio Cannavaro left the club, many of their key men decided to stay and earn Juventus's promotion back to Serie A. Italians Alessandro Del Piero and Gianluigi Buffon had won the World Cup that summer but elected to remain with 'The Old Lady' in the second tier. They were joined by David Trezeguet and Pavel Nedvěd, who helped blood a group of young players who included Sebastian Giovinco and Claudio Marchisio.

That 2006/07 season saw Juventus win promotion back to Italy's Serie A. Despite their deduction of nine points, Juve stormed the second division, helped by 20 goals from Del Piero as they won the title with three matches to spare. Their final points tally of 85 put them six clear of second-placed Napoli and their quest would begin again for Italian dominance. With Claudio Ranieri appointed manager, Juve would finish third in their first season back and qualify for the Champions League.

Juventus would take a long while to shake off the stench of scandal. The Old Lady was hit far harder than any of her rivals. Despite this, in recent years *Calciopoli* is a distant memory of the club. Juventus have failed to legally reclaim those two titles that were stripped from them, but in recent years they have added eight consecutive *Scudettos* to their historic trophy cabinet. Milan have never really recovered from the scandal. The squad in recent seasons has missed out on Champions League qualification and seen Juve grow stronger and stronger. For Moggi, the only way to stop the *Bianconeri* is another *Calciopoli*.[270]

---

270 Luciano Moggi on *Twitter* (8 October 2018)

43

David Beckham Joins LA Galaxy (2007)

Sportsmen and women over the decades have become household names. In fact, at times they have been even more famous than politicians, monarchs and television celebrities. The names Muhammed Ali, Usain Bolt and Serena Williams are arguably known by even those who are vehemently opposed to both watching and reading about sports. In football the names Lionel Messi and Cristiano Ronaldo are well known around the world, but there is one former professional who arguably surpasses even these two greats of the game. The man in question is, of course, David Beckham.

A member of the 'class of 92', he made his name in Sir Alex Ferguson's Manchester United side. Perhaps the key to his fame was his front-page relationship with Spice Girl Victoria Adams. Never out of the footballing spotlight since his goal against Wimbledon (from his own half), by the 1998 World Cup he was already one of the game's biggest names. A red card in the last 16 against bitter rivals Argentina would turn public opinion against him, however. In a competition where the young and refreshing Michael Owen had made headlines for his goals and 'good boy' image, Beckham's celebrity was seen as a prime reason for his failings on the pitch.[271]

---

271 Chris Flanagan, 'When David Beckham was the most hated man in England', *FourFourTwo* (20 August 2018)

For many, such an incident could have ended a promising career, but for Beckham it became the source of his resurgence on the world stage. Despite ridiculous death threats and widespread public animosity, he would later describe the moment as one of the top five in his career. Tripping Diego Simeone in Saint-Etienne helped to change the future England captain on and off the pitch.[272] The next season, Beckham was instrumental in helping United win an historic treble. His status would grow off the pitch as a result, but on it he continued to improve, even finishing second in the FIFA World Player of the Year in 1999.

In 2001, now captain of the national team, 'Goldenballs' would take England to the World Cup following a stoppage-time trademark free kick against Greece. Meeting England in the group stage in Korea and Japan was Argentina. Just before half-time in Sapporo, Beckham smashed home a penalty to make amends for his error four years previous. Propelled to even greater heights of fame, he would earn a multi-million pound move to the *Galacticos* of Real Madrid. Beckham-mania was in full swing.

Surprisingly, his stint in Spain was not as trophy-laden as it should have been. A single La Liga between 2003 and 2007 meant rumours began to spread that he may be looking for a new club. At only 32, however, and still seemingly at a high level, it came as a surprise when his transfer to LA Galaxy was announced. In 2007 the MLS was lacking any international publicity and an absence of quality made it unappealing to many footballers.

For Beckham, the opportunity was incredible. With charities and contacts already set up across the pond, joining LA was a natural step. Despite offers from European and British teams, his heart was set on the move. In a BBC article on the announcement of Beckham's move, LA Galaxy

---

272 Freddie Campion, ' David Beckham: World Cup Red One of My Top Career Moments', *GQ* (18 March 2016)

manager Alexi Lalas was clear in his belief that the signing would have a huge impact on US soccer. Likewise, president of owners AEG, Timothy J Leiweke, was reported to have said, 'David Beckham will have a greater impact on soccer in America than any athlete has ever had on a sport globally.'[273] But was he right?

From his arrival, the media attention and boost for the league was clear to see. Immediately, sponsorship deals and investments were commonplace in the league. Stadiums and spectatorship rose dramatically, creating, for perhaps the first time, a genuinely glamorous league in the United States. By the time Beckham left Los Angeles in 2012, the average attendance at MLS games had risen from 15,504 in 2006 to 18,807. Furthermore, the total attendance had improved from just under three million to a remarkable six million in the same period.[274] This can be traced to the increase in fixtures but what this also shows is that the league had grown and the appetite for soccer in the States was at its greatest level.

What was more impressive was Beckham's attitude once he arrived. He could have been forgiven for playing out his career in the MLS, but in reality he went on to win a number of major trophies. Two MLS Cups and two Supporters Shields later, his legacy was secure. In a review of Beckham's time in LA by *The Guardian* in 2017, they drew particular attention to this.[275] Described as a 'fierce competitor', his performances both on and off the pitch during his five-year spell helped to improve the league considerably.

273 'Beckham agrees to LA Galaxy move', *BBC Sport* (12 January 2007) http://news.bbc.co.uk/sport1/hi/football/6248835.stm

274 'Major League Soccer – Attendance Figures', *Transfer Markt* (2012) https://www.transfermarkt.co.uk/major-league-soccer/besucherzahlen/wettbewerb/MLS1/plus/?saison_id=2011

275 Kristian Heneage, 'A decade on, did David Beckham's move to MLS make a difference?', *The Guardian* (11 January 2017) https://www.theguardian.com/football/blog/2017/jan/11/david-beckham-la-galaxy-mls

Perhaps Beckham's only negative was in his loan moves to Milan during the winter break in 2009 and 2010. For some, Beckham's good form for Galaxy and a potential 2010 World Cup place up for grabs meant he would be looking for a permanent move back to Europe. Despite a successful initial spell, the midfielder was clear in his intent to return to LA. However, this wasn't what many Galaxy fans believed. Indeed, on his return, Beckham was met with boos from some sections of the home crowd. Perhaps not helped by some harsh words from captain Landon Donovan, some supporters were quick to describe him as a part-time player.[276]

This moment truly shows the power of the footballer. We have already seen how tremendously influential the game is as a whole – but certain individuals from within the sport can make a difference by themselves. Beckham, in some ways, is *the* modern sportsperson. Although throughout sports history certain athletes have been highly revered and even idolised, Beckham reflects the celebrity of modern football. There was seldom a moment in his long and successful career that wasn't splashed upon the back and often front pages. What was ultimately refreshing to see was that Beckham used his status to promote the game in the US. With Zlatan Ibrahimovic, Wayne Rooney and Steven Gerrard all following Beckham to the US, his legacy and influence is clear to see.

---

276 'Beckham confronts fans after boos', *BBC Sport* (20 July 2009) http://news.bbc.co.uk/sport1/hi/football/8158547.stm

44

Tiki-Taka (2008)

Earlier in this book, we took a closer look at the 'dream team' of Johan Cruyff at Barcelona. Cruyff's side and their prosperity was manufactured by an incredibly successful mixture of possession and quick passing. Following this, football styles continued to develop and change. Italian *catenaccio* had re-emerged to become integral to the Milan and Juventus European triumphs, before Real Madrid's team of superstars dominated the continent at the turn of the century. A tactical revolution was about to begin.

Utilised across the Iberian peninsula, a new brand of football called 'tiki-taka' would be meticulously planned and developed in Catalonia.

It is perhaps easiest to break this moment into two distinct parts. Firstly, the Spanish national team, under the stewardship of Luis Aragonés, would remove the tag of 'perennial underachievers', before Pep Guardiola's Barcelona took the tactical style to new realms of dominance at the turn of the decade.

Following on from Cruyff's vision of a unified Barcelona side on the Catalan coast, few could foresee the invincible aura Pep's side would produce. The global superiority of both Spain and Barcelona would bring into question just who was the greatest international and club side of all time.

Spain

Step forward Luis Aragonés – 'The wise man of Hortaleza'. Following defeat to France at the 2006 World Cup, Aragonés would introduce a new style of football to the national team – tiki-taka. Characterised by quick, short-distance passes, the tactical change would promote movement and possession over route-one play. It seemed that keeping possession of the ball took precedence over scoring goals.[277] Teams who would attempt to defend against it would be worn out as the ball zipped around the pitch with players drifting into each and every position. Leadership of the team was with the midfielders, notably Xavi and Andres Iniesta.[278]

Spain cruised through the group stage and met world champions Italy in the quarter-finals. Xavi bossed the game, providing the pivot in midfield, 'caressing the ball one way and then the other, all one-touch passing with quick bursts of activity'.[279] Despite a 0-0 draw, *La Roja* would win on penalties. In terms of shoot-outs, history had been unkind to the Spanish, who even lost one to England in 1996. But when Cesc Fabregas fired passed Gianluigi Buffon, Spain had cast aside the notions of underachievers and emerged as a force one again.

Russia were beaten in the semis, and the final of a major tournament, for the first time since 1960, was to feature a Spanish XI. Even with an injury to top goalscorer David Villa, the BBC believed they could still do it. 'Veteran coach Luis Aragonés now looks to have put together a side capable of ending the years of under-achievement, even making light of that injury to the influential Villa.'[280] Spain would meet Germany in the final, with Torres sent out as a lone striker as

277 Josh Faga, *The Real Giants of Soccer Coaching: Insights and Wisdom from the Game's Great Coaches* (Maidenhead: Meyer and Meyer, 2018) p.223

278 Guillem Balague, *Pep Guardiola: Another Way of Winning: The Biography* (London, Hachette, 2018)

279 John Atkin, 'Casillas's saves put Spain in semis', *UEFA* (23 June 2008)

280 Phil McNulty, 'Russia 0-3 Spain', *BBC Sport* (26 June 2008)

their usual 4-4-2 was adapted to a 4-1-4-1 to cover for Villa's injury and to combat Germany's 4-2-3-1. The change worked, Torres scored the winner in the 33rd minute and *La Roja's* tiki-taka won them Euro 2008 with nine of their squad selected for 'Team of the Tournament'.

Barcelona

Aragonés left his job with Spain straight after victory in Vienna. Although inventing the style, its next great innovator would come in the shape of Pep Guardiola. In his playing career, Guardiola had been a key cog in the 1992 Dream Team under Johan Cruyff. Following a successful season coaching Barcelona's 'B' side, he was brought in to replace Frank Rijkaard at the Camp Nou. The myth that many people believe is that Guardiola was thrown into an already complete team of champions. Not so. In fact, in 2008 Barcelona had finished third in La Liga, over 20 points behind bitter rivals Real Madrid. Despite European success in 2006, the squad had become disgruntled. Talented individuals like Ronaldinho and Deco were instantly sold, with Guardiola looking for players who could play in line with the philosophy the club had developed under Cruyff.[281]

Guardiola was quick to train his team with quick passing drills and introduced painstakingly intricate analysis of the opposition. Together with never-before-seen levels of possession, his side would pass the enemy to death, before attacking with speed and dynamism. Leading from Cruyff's example, it was not uncommon for Guardiola to stop a training match in order to correct and explain what could have been done better.[282] If the pitch at the Camp Nou was for winning, the training ground was certainly for learning. Sergio Busquets

281 Seb Stafford-Bloor, 'La Masia: The History of Barcelona's Academy', *Tifo Football* (18 September 2019) https://www.youtube.com/watch?v=tResxp9hOHo

282 Guillem Balague, *Pep Guardiola: Another Way of Winning: The Biography* (London, Hachette, 2018)

had been one of Guardiola's finest pupils at Barcelona 'B' and was immediately promoted from the fourth division in Spanish football to the first team XI.

In his first full season as manager, his revolutionary style blew the opposition away. Barcelona won the treble. La Liga was won by nine points from Real Madrid, who they had beaten earlier in the 6-2 at the Bernabeu. In a match dubbed by *Marca* as 'Guardiola's masterpiece', central to the victory was 21-year-old Lionel Messi.[283] This was the first time Guardiola had used the Argentine in the 'false nine' role. Messi wasn't a recognised striker and even with proven goalscorers Thierry Henry and Samuel Eto'o in the side, he was positioned as a deep-lying forward. In this way, he could drop between the lines with Henry and Eto'o running in from the wing. With the ever-present Xavi and Iniesta dominating the midfield, the side would go from strength to strength.

The peak of the *Blaugrana's* powers, however, was in 2011. It is widely accepted that this team is arguably the greatest in history. Rivals Real Madrid attempted to stem the flow of trophies, heading to the Nou Camp by hiring tactical antithesis Jose Mourinho as manager. In the first *Clasico* since the special one's arrival, Barca produced one of the best 90-minute performances in history. Messi, Villa, Iniesta and Xavi ripped *Los Blancos* to shreds. Barcelona 5-0 Real Madrid. The superlatives used from the thousands of journalists watching around the world perhaps say it best. 'Barcelona were out of this world tonight, it's one of the most perfect team performances you could ever wish to see.'[284]

That season, Guardiola's side would go on to win a remarkable La Liga and Champions League. La Liga was won by four points and the Champions League was secured

---

283 Miguel Angel Lara, 'Barcelona's 6-2 win over Real Madrid: Guardiola's masterpiece', *Marca* (17 August 2018)

284 Jonathan Stevenson, 'Barcelona v Real Madrid as it happened', *BBC Sport* (29 November 2010) http://news.bbc.co.uk/sport1/hi/football/9239226.stm

after another virtuoso performance which drew praise from football fans across the globe. Beating Manchester United 3-1 at Wembley, opposition manager Sir Alex Ferguson was quick to admit his side were 'mesmerised' by the tiki-taka passing. For Ferguson, Barcelona played the game in the 'right way'.[285]

Tiki-taka's legacy was secure. Alongside Barcelona, the Spanish national team was also continuing to dominate. Going in to the 2010 World Cup, they had only lost one in 48 matches. The tournament itself showcased once more the effectiveness of 'tiki-taka' on the opposition. Following a fierce and ill-disciplined final, Andres Iniesta struck a late winner. Two years later, the side attempted back-to-back European triumphs – something no other nation had done. A virtuoso campaign saw *La Roja* reach the final, where they thumped Italy 4-0. It was the peak of the Spanish powers and teams would have to totally reinvent their tactics to beat them. This was football at its purest. Football we know and football we love.

---

285 Sir Alex Ferguson press conference, 28 May 2011

45

The World Cup Arrives in Africa (2010)

Football, as we have seen, has had the power to bring people together from all around the world. Earlier moments have shown how the game quickly became incredibly popular in Europe and South America, before spreading to other continents. The late 1980s and early 1990s had seen a rise in African football.

Despite a modern history full of exploitation, dictatorial governments and poverty, in a footballing sense, the wins for Cameroon at the 1990 World Cup and later Senegal provided evidence of an emerging game. When South Africa won the right to host the biggest competition on Earth, it was sure to raise a few eyebrows. For most, it was the culmination of 20 years of growth in African football.

As FIFA continuously expanded and the World Cup grew to cater for more sides, African sides, for the first time, were given a platform on the biggest stage of all. Despite Egypt's appearance at the 1934 tournament, the former colonisation of the African continent meant it would be another 36 years before a team qualified – this time Morocco. Subsequent performances from nations like Zaire failed to make much of an impact, until the 1990 World Cup. Cameroon's run to the quarter-finals that year earned the respect and praise of people all around the world. For the first time, Africa was being noticed.

The star of the show was Roger Milla. At 36 he had scored three goals to help his nation progress. In 1994 and 1998, the progression of African sides continued with the Super Eagles of Nigeria impressing many in the latter. By now the tournament was catering for 32 teams, of which five would be from Africa. In the opening game of the 2002 World Cup, relative unknowns Senegal beat holders France 1-0. Overnight, Senegalese heroes Diouf, Diao and Diop were household names.

The time seemed right for an African nation to host the competition. In 2006 South Africa had narrowly missed out to Germany by a single vote. Following the disappointment, president of FIFA Sepp Blatter was determined to bring the tournament to the African continent. Proposing that the World Cup hosts should be rotated by continent, the five bids for 2010 came from the aforementioned South Africa, Morocco, Tunisia/Libya, Egypt and Nigeria. South Africa was awarded the honour of hosting despite reports that Morocco had in fact received more votes.[286] In the subsequent years, allegations of bribery and corruption, in regards to the awarding of the World Cup to South Africa, have been rife.

For all their discrepancies, FIFA had put vast amounts of money and resources into the continent in the years leading up to 2010, and now was the chance to showcase it to the globe. South Africa seemed the natural hosts following their 1990s rebirth. From 1961 to 1992, the nation had not been allowed to compete against their African and world rivals due to a FIFA ban. After decades of strict race-driven apartheid rule, the resulting emancipation of Nelson Mandela and the resulting 1995 Rugby World Cup success had bolstered national unity.[287]

---

286 *The Telegraph*, 6 June 2015

287 Peter Alegi and Chris Bolsmann (eds), *Africa's World Cup: Critical Reflections on Play, Patriotism, Spectatorship and Space* (Michigan: University of Michigan, 2013) p.4

African culture was to be central to the tournament. A culture which throughout history has often been stifled was now able to flourish under the gaze of over half a billion people. The venue for the final, nicknamed 'Soccer City', was architecturally designed to represent a *calabash* (an African pot). It was these subtle themes, together with the more blatant *vuvuzela* that celebrated all things African. The stadiums, fans and locations helped create a marvellous atmosphere – a true carnival of football was about to begin.

In hindsight, the 2010 World Cup will not be remembered for the football. In fact, the overall quality was actually rather poor. The final between the Netherlands and Spain showcased the game at its most unfriendly, contrary to the atmosphere amongst supporters in Johannesburg. Spain emerged victorious following a late Andres Iniesta goal in extra time. The match itself had seen a record 14 yellow cards and a red handed to Dutchman Johnny Heitinga. The tiki-taka style, which had been so successful for Vicente Del Bosque's side, was ruthlessly cut down by cynical and often outrageous tackles. Nigel De Jong's 'kung-fu' kick on Xabi Alonso stands out as a particularly brutal piece of play.

What the first African World Cup will be remembered for is what it meant to an entire continent. There is no hiding from the corruption scandal which plagued its awarding, but in bringing the World Cup to Africa it showed that football truly is a universal game for everyone. It showed that it has the power to inspire people, no matter what their socio-economic situation dictates. Football truly is the world's language.

2012-Present

46

Aguerooooo!!! (2012)

This moment is one of my favourite moments in the list; it was absolutely sensational! In a house in Swansea with six or so Manchester United supporters, myself (a Cardiff fan) and an Everton fan were the only two wanting Man City to win the Premier League. When Sky Sports commentator Martin Tyler screamed that now famous word, 'AGUEROOOOO!', I will never, ever forget the unbelievable joy and delirium I experienced. Hugging and dancing around the living room with the Everton fan, the devastation of the surrounding United fans!

It had nothing to do with wanting United to lose the league, it was just the astonishingly, stunningly brilliant finish to a Premier League season – like nothing else I'd ever seen! It's a moment that still gets the heart racing and gives goosebumps to this very day, wow!

Roberto Mancini's Manchester City were hunting their first-ever Premier League title, their first top-flight title since 1967/68 and only their third ever. Chairman Khaldoon Al Mubarak had invested heavily in the Citizens in the pursuit of Premier League glory and the summer of 2011 saw the additions of Samir Nasri, Gaël Clichy and notably Sergio 'Kun' Agüero. Agüero, the £40m signing from Atlético Madrid, joined with a reputation for goals already. At 23, Kun had the best of his career ahead of him and immediately sought to prove himself in England with 23 top-flight goals to match his age in his debut campaign.

City started the season on fire, 12 wins and two draws taking them to 12 December before they tasted defeat in the league. In that time, they had already recorded another historic victory – 6-1 at Old Trafford versus fierce title rivals Manchester United. That famous day was also watched at that same house in Swansea, with those same Manchester United fans. Of course, it is the day Mario Balotelli pulled out his 'Why Always Me?' t-shirt, a jibe at the media who had hounded the Italian since his arrival at the Etihad. City made a statement that day that would take them through the rest of the season with just four defeats to their name. A second victory versus Manchester United in April, with just three matches left of the season, would set up a grandstand finish to the title race.

13 May 2012 – Manchester City hosted QPR on the last day of the season; Manchester United, meanwhile, were away to Sunderland. Right-back Pablo Zabaleta gave City the lead in the 39th minute in a game they needed to win to become champions. 1-0 at half-time and City were looking strong, but just three minutes into the second half and QPR frontman Djibril Cissé struck to level the tie. Joey Barton, QPR captain, then caught Carlos Tevez with a swinging elbow in the 55th minute. He was shown a red card before lashing out with a kick aimed at Agüero and a head-butt aimed at Vincent Kompany – the less said about Monsieur Barton the better! However, the red was not a turning point for City. QPR struck again through Jamie Mackie and led 2-1.

QPR were battling relegation themselves but were saved as Stoke drew with Bolton to relegate the Trotters. Manchester United won their match at Sunderland courtesy of Wayne Rooney and with the game running behind at the Etihad due to the red card, many City fans were leaving the stadium in tears – had they blown their title shot? Then in the 92nd minute, a David Silva corner found the head of Edin Džeko to level it, 2-2! City threw everything forwards in the last seconds of added time – had they left it too late?

Suddenly, 94 minutes in, Agüero picked the ball up 30 yards out. He played it to Balotelli, who slipped but managed to find Agüero, who had continued his forward run. Kun took it past his defender and smashed it past Paddy Kenny in the QPR net – 'AGUEROOOOO!' 3-2! City had won the league, United were left devastated and the Premier League had one of its greatest-ever moments!

'The only word to describe it is bedlam' reported *The Guardian*,[288] whilst the *Daily Mail* wrote philosophically, 'What can never be captured on the black and white pages of the record books is the effect this day will have on all those who were present.'[289] In the short term, the moment became transformational for the Citizens, a new era had arrived. Martin Tyler recalls how his commentary led 'the City megastore to run out of "O"s due to all of the "Agueroooo" shirts printed', with fans being desperate to commemorate history.[290] The longer-term impact has seen City surpass United as Manchester's leading club at present. Another title followed in 2013/14 before the appointment of Pep Guardiola earned City back-to-back wins in 2017/18 and 2018/19. The 'noisy neighbours',[291] as Sir Alex Ferguson once termed them, are seemingly here to stay, with no intention of turning the noise down!

288 *The Guardian*, 13 May 2012

289 *Daily Mail*, 13 May 2012

290 *The Telegraph*, 20 December 2012

291 *Metro*, 20 September 2009

47

2014 FIFA World Cup – Brazil 1-7 Germany (2014)

In 2014 Brazil hosted the FIFA World Cup, their first time hosting since 1950. Neymar, 22, Brazil's talisman was the poster boy of the tournament, the hopes of a football-besotted nation resting on his young shoulders. Lionel Messi, meanwhile, was attempting to win his first World Cup with Brazil's rivals Argentina as the German side were the most fancied team to feature from Europe. In a competition boasting 171 goals in just 64 matches (2.67 per game), the semi-final clash between Brazil and Germany will never be forgotten.

The Brazilians, in 2014, had a very clear aim, banish the pain of *Maracanazo* (Moment 16). Back in 1950, Brazil were expected to win the World Cup on home soil. However, a stunning defeat by Uruguay led to tears, anger and even 'stadium doctors treating 169 people for fits of hysteria', with 'six taken to hospital seriously ill'.[292] Just the second time the nation had the privilege of hosting the tournament, the *Seleção* were once again being touted as the side to watch that glorious summer – could they lift the trophy for a sixth time?

Brazil's route to the last four was an eventful one. Falling behind to Croatia in their opener, thanks to a Marcelo own

---

292 *The Guardian*, 15 March 2018

goal, it took superstar Neymar to score a brace to put Brazil ahead. Oscar rounded off the game in added time to secure a 3-1 victory. A draw with Mexico and a win over Cameroon set up a last-16 fixture with Chile. The all-South American tie would go to penalties after a 1-1 draw, with Neymar netting the final spot-kick for the hosts – a scare had been survived!

In the quarter-finals, Brazil would face more South Americans – Colombia. James Rodríguez had been in superb form for the Colombians thus far, the 23-year-old going on to win the Golden Boot, Goal of the Tournament and the 2014 FIFA Puskás Award for his World Cup efforts. Rodríguez's 80th-minute penalty was in vain, though, as Brazilian defenders Thiago Silva and David Luiz both scored to put the *Seleção* into a huge semi-final clash with Germany.

Germany started their campaign with an excellent 4-0 victory over Cristiano Ronaldo's Portugal, a hat-trick from Thomas Müller adding to a goal from centre-back Mats Hummels. A gripping 2-2 draw with Ghana was followed by a 1-0 win over the USA, and the Germans were into the last 16 as group winners. A 0-0 draw with Algeria in normal time was unexpected but André Schürrle and Mesut Özil both netted in extra time to put Germany through, despite Djabou responding for Algeria. Germany and France met in a European quarter-final and Dortmund defender Hummels scored again for his country – Germany would meet Brazil, mouth-watering!

On 8 July 2014, Brazil would host Germany in Belo Horizonte. Devastatingly for Brazil, Neymar had picked up an injury in their win over Colombia that would rule him out of the rest of the World Cup. The broken vertebrae in his back was seemingly the culmination of heavy challenges laid on Neymar throughout the competition, team-mate Hulk saying, 'Every time is like this. Players always come after Neymar. The referees need to do more to keep this from happening.'[293]

---

293 *The Telegraph*, 5 July 2014

Luiz Felipe Scolari's men would have to do it without their main man.

Settling down in the pub where I watched this game in Cardiff, I was not expecting what happened next! The Germans set a blistering pace: Müller (11), Miroslav Klose (23), Toni Kroos (24 and 26), Sami Khedira (29) – Germany had blown the hosts away and led 5-0 after just 29 minutes. The pub was stunned, the Estádio Mineirão was rocked – fans crying as their dream World Cup crumbled. Following the break, Germany maintained control of the fixture and even added two more thanks to a Schürrle brace. Despite Oscar's consolation goal, the 7-1 defeat reverberated around the footballing world.

The humiliation was dubbed the *Mineirazo*, a new and even more shameful *Maracanazo* with the Germans described as playing 'football as blood sport'.[294] It was said that the Brazilian nation would spend 'the rest of their lives grieving about Tuesday, 8 July [2014], the day that Brazilian football was demolished in one of its own great cities'.[295] The World Cup that had promised so much had now fallen apart in staggering style.

Brazil would not recover in time for the third-place play-off match against the Netherlands; a 3-0 loss would mean the hosts finished their home World Cup in fourth place. Germany's well-earned final would be against another South American team – Argentina. Leo Messi was hunting that elusive World Cup that he craved so badly to emulate Diego Maradona. In the famous Maracanã Stadium, five days after their mighty victory, Germany played out a 0-0 draw with Argentina in normal time. Extra time was a tense affair, until, in the 113th minute, Mario Götze of Bayern Munich netted the winning strike. Germany lifted the trophy, their fourth, as they broke the hearts of yet more South Americans. What a World Cup 2014 will be remembered as!

---

294 *The Guardian*, 23 May 2018
295 *The Independent*, 9 July 2014

48

Leicester City Win the Premier League (2015/16)

Whilst Agüero's moment (Moment 46) was the best finish to a Premier League campaign ever, Leicester City in 2015/16 is perhaps the greatest season in the Premier League era. Since the new-style top flight began in 1992, Manchester United and Arsenal had dominated the title-winners' list. The addition of José Mourinho to the Premier League had seen Chelsea added to the competitors and of course Manchester City were always going to be there or thereabouts too, backed by huge financial investment. The only surprise in over 20 years stood out as Blackburn in 1994/95; however, Leicester City were about to dramatically change things.

In 2014/15 newly promoted Leicester spent most of the season in the relegation zone. Nigel Pearson's men survived the drop and managed to finish in 14th position. The Leicester board felt a change was needed and former Chelsea head coach Claudio Ranieri was the man they elected for that role in the summer of 2015. Ranieri's appointment caused some controversy amongst Leicester fans, *Match of the Day* host Gary Lineker tweeting, 'Claudio Ranieri? Really?'[296] *The Guardian,*

---

296 Tweeted from his personal Twitter account [@GaryLineker] on 13 July 2015

meanwhile, called Claudio the 'wrong man' in a scathing article that cited his recent failures with the Greek national team: 'poor is perhaps an understatement in the circumstances'.[297] Ranieri's most recent success had come in Ligue 2 of France with Monaco, promoting them as champions in 2012/13, but what could the Italian do with the Foxes?

Ranieri's first signing was N'Golo Kanté, the defensive midfielder from Caen, for £5.6m, a relative unknown. Kanté joined the additions of Christian Fuchs, Robert Huth, Shinji Okazaki, Yohan Benalouane and Gökhan Inler. Pre-season, Leicester were (now famously) given odds of 5,000/1 to win the league. Claudio's job was certainly to keep the Foxes into the top flight rather than win it. Their campaign started fairly solidly, three wins and three draws taking them into September before they tasted their first defeat, a 5-2 home demolition by Arsenal, with talisman Jamie Vardy scoring twice in that loss. Perhaps the embarrassment spurred Leicester on though, because after that the team went undefeated until Boxing Day, picking up eight wins and two draws.

During this first half of the season, Jamie Vardy broke a Premier League record for most consecutive goals after he netted in 11 matches in a row. Making himself a fantasy football dream, Vardy's run stretched from a 1-1 draw with Bournemouth on 29 August with an 86th-minute penalty to a stunning counter-attack goal in a 1-1 draw with Manchester United on 28 November. Vardy's rise became the stuff of English footballing folklore. A former factory worker for a manufacturer of prosthetic limbs,[298] Vardy came to Leicester via Stocksbridge Park Steels, Halifax Town and Fleetwood Town – not exactly the route expected of a Premier League winner! His 24 for the season was a major factor in Leicester's threat from the counter-attack; his speed and a prolific nature made him feared by Premier League defenders in 2015/16.

---

297 *The Guardian*, 14 July 2015
298 *Yorkshire Post*, 17 September 2017

Leicester's squad that year was full of unlikely heroes: Kanté proved a genius signing in breaking up play for Ranieri's men, whilst Riyad Mahrez (a 2014 signing for less than £1m) was scintillating in securing that year's PFA Player of the Season awards. Jamaican defender and Foxes captain Wes Morgan's partnership with Robert Huth was unbreakable too. All year Leicester were only defeated three times, by Arsenal home and away and by Liverpool at Anfield 1-0. Their relentless discipline saw them win seven games 1-0 and 14 of their 23 wins were by a margin of just one goal. As the season headed into its closing stages, no one could quite believe what they were seeing, Leicester's run to the title just kept on rolling. The crown was eventually wrapped up as Tottenham drew 2-2 at Chelsea on 2 May 2016, and the party could begin. Their final points score of 81 was ten clear of runners-up Arsenal – a magnificent achievement in a season that will never be forgotten, a season for the underdogs!

Dozens of stories cropped up across the UK of fans taking the bookies' odds of 5,000/1 for Leicester to win the league. It was described as the 'icing on the cake' for gamblers, with one bet winning as much as £112,500; the total outlay costing the betting industry between '£10-20 million'.[299] However, it wasn't just the financial excitement of a Foxes win; the delight was country-wide as the Premier League showed it could still provide a sizable shock – even in the world of super-BSkyB funding and the 'top six'!

Sadly, the story does not end there, as two years later a tragic accident followed involving a key man behind the Leicester success. On 27 October 2018 Leicester City owner and facilitator of the title win Vichai Srivaddhanaprabha was killed in a helicopter crash. Vichai was well known for taking off in a helicopter from the club's ground, the King Power Stadium, after matches. Tragedy struck in 2018, though, after a draw with West Ham United. Reports emerged of a

---

299 *Daily Mail*, 3 May 2016

helicopter crash outside the ground that evening as Vichai and four other people died in the incident. The club united in grief and the next week recorded an emotional 1-0 win at Cardiff City. Vichai's contribution to the city of Leicester will never be forgotten and he will be immortalised forever in the hearts of Leicester fans who remember the great 2015/16 season at the King Power Stadium.

49

Chapecoense Disaster (2016)

Football and tragedy seem to cross paths far too often. The Munich Air Disaster in 1958 (Moment 20) that involved Manchester United was an horrifically sad story that decimated a very promising young side. Likewise, the Superga disaster of 1949 (Moment 15) saw five-time Italian champions Grande Torino wiped out in a terrible air crash. In 2016 a similar story broke on 28 November, and this time it involved a promising Brazilian football team, Chapecoense. The plane that crashed, LaMia flight 2933, carried 77 people; 71 of these passengers lost their lives that fateful night. The death toll included footballers, coaching staff and journalists alike travelling to the first leg of the final of the Copa Sudamericana in Medellin, Colombia.

Chapecoense had enjoyed a meteoric rise to Brazil's Série A. In 2009 the side were playing in the fourth tier, Série D, before earning their promotion to Série C and then in 2013 Série B. They spent just one season in the second tier, coming in second place and earning promotion to Brazil's top flight. The side had managed to consolidate their Série A status and in 2015 and then again in 2016 featured in CONMEBOL's version of the UEFA Europa League (second-tier continental tournament). In 2016 this run had led them all the way to the two-leg final against Colombian outfit Atlético Nacional.

Chapecoense were flying from Santa Cruz de la Sierra, Bolivia, to Medellin, Colombia. They had seen off Brazilian side Cuiabá, Argentinian teams Independiente and San Lorenzo and Colombians Junior en route to their first-ever continental cup final. On 28 November, with the flight running behind schedule, it was decided that the plane would skip a refuelling stop. This decision had devastating consequences as the fuel levels ran critically low; this, in turn, was hurt by air traffic control at Medellin Airport, who prioritised other planes landing ahead of LaMia flight 2933. A final error occurred when there was a failure to call in the emergency in time as the plane descended rapidly.[300]

Of the 22 players on board the plane that day, just three survived – left-back Alan Ruschel, centre-back Neto and back-up goalkeeper Jakson Follmann. Follmann unfortunately had one of his legs amputated due to his injuries and was forced to retire from professional sport.[301] In the aftermath of the disaster, Atlético Nacional petitioned CONMEBOL to award Chapecoense the Copa Sudamericana. This was granted, along with the prize money for the tournament and a place in next season's Copa Libertadores (the top-tier continental competition).

Brazilian and Argentinian football united to support Chapecoense, offering to loan out players to them for free. Clubs also sent a joint request to the Brazilian FA asking for Chapecoense to be exempt from relegation for three years. Chapecoense, though, rejected all offers of assistance and stated that they wanted to rebuild their club properly. In the 2017 campaign, Chapecoense were not unwilling to make changes to ensure their place in Série A was secure, managers

---

300 BBC, 'Colombia Chapecoense plane crash: What we know', *BBC News* (9 December 2016) https://www.bbc.co.uk/news/world-latin-america-38142998

301 Tim Vickery, 'Chapecoense plane crash: How the club is still defying the odds one year on', *BBC Sport* (27 November 2017) https://www.bbc.co.uk/sport/football/42137506

Vagner Mancini and Vinícius Eutrópio being sacked after poor runs of results. However, Chape sealed survival from relegation with an emotional 2-1 victory over Vitoria with four games to spare. Their new side had done the seemingly impossible and were joined in the feat by Neto and Ruschel, both recovering from their crash injuries, to play once again.

In 2018 a 14th-place finish was achieved but, sadly for the Chapecoense fans, 2019 would see the end of their top-flight stay. A difficult season on the pitch was added to by numerous managerial changes, and the courageous Chapecoense could survive no longer. The 2016 air disaster, though, had brought tears to many South Americans and opened the eyes of modern football fans to the reality that footballers, their heroes, are mortal. When new Cardiff City signing Emiliano Sala was also killed in an air accident in January 2019, this feeling was further compounded. Bill Shankly's famous words that football is more important than life and death are perhaps not so accurate when considered in the midst of tragedy.

Vamos Chape!

50

Video Assistant Referees – VAR (2018)

Video Assistant Referees (VAR) – probably one of the most talked-about things in football since 2018, and the culmination of years of debate. Video technology is now well used in sports throughout the world: tennis, cricket, American football, rugby league, rugby union, field hockey and ice hockey too. Football had long been resistant to the introduction of video referrals that could overrule the on-pitch match official. However, in the 2010 World Cup, after Frank Lampard had a clearly legitimate goal ruled out against Germany, goal-line technology was developed and introduced. This was successful and swept across each country's association, mainly due to the lack of noticeability during a game – a simple watch the referee wore to let him know if a goal had been scored. Video replays though? Far, far more controversial!

Video technology was first trialled by the Dutch Football Association (KNVB) in the 2012/13 Eredivisie season, but only in mock trials. The USA then took on the system in 2016 reserve matches, the first red and yellow cards being issued because of it. A friendly between France and Italy in September 2016 became the first international match to use the system in more trials, before the Australian A-League took the step to use it in the first competitive top-flight fixture in the world. MLS adopted the system likewise in their 2017 campaign, and Russia's FIFA Confederations Cup in June 2017 also used the developing system.

Bundesliga (Germany) and Serie A (Italy) agreed to use VAR for the 2017/18 season before the big confirmation came that the 2018 World Cup in Russia would feature video assistants. With the International Football Association Board (IFAB) officially writing VAR into the rules of the game, in Britain plenty of fans, journalists and ex-pros alike were still unconvinced.

The first use in the UK came in a January 2018 FA Cup clash between Brighton and Crystal Palace. The debate surrounded the extent to which VAR could be used, the four calls detailed as: goals featuring offsides or fouls, penalty decisions, direct red card decisions (second yellow cards not being reviewable) or mistaken identity in awarding a red or yellow card. The problem many fans had was the length of time reviews were taking at pitchside monitors and the confusion it caused in the stadiums. José Mourinho commented in February 2018, 'The referees should decide on VAR. Do they feel happy with it? Do they want some technical help? Or do they still want to live with the human mistakes they make?'[302]

So we come to the 2018 FIFA World Cup in Russia. VAR would be the biggest tournament talking point with the phrase 'clear and obvious error' ringing in everyone's ears. This was to be the point at which reviews would take place. The men watching in the booths in Moscow (in full refereeing kit too) would communicate with the on-pitch official to recommend he review a decision. For the most part, VAR seemed to be a success, reviews done quickly allowing errors to be corrected. It was reported after the group stages: '335 incidents were checked – nearly seven per game – with 14 on-field reviews made by referees and three reviews made by the VAR team

---

302 *Daily Mirror*, 17 February 2018

on factual decisions.' It was stated that referees called '95 per cent' of incidents correctly without the intervention of VAR, but with VAR included it 'improved the success rate to 99.3 per cent'.[303]

Debate about VAR still continues to rage. Some fans expect instant perfection and when VAR does not provide that, it is therefore seen as a failure. Some fans also believed calls had become too 'soft' in 2018, a handball during a match between Portugal and Iran led to players agreeing with this. However, VAR is seemingly here to stay across the footballing world and has helped correct many 'clear and obvious errors' since 2018, as well as many more minor errors too.

On 15 November 2018, after a number of poor refereeing decisions that would otherwise have been VAR adjusted, the Premier League became the last of Europe's top-five leagues to confirm its introduction from the 2019/20 season. In the opening months of the 2019/20 campaign, criticism was thrown at the system by fans. English referees separated themselves from their European counterparts by setting a 'high bar' for VAR intervention, meaning many incidents were left 'uncorrected' in spectators' eyes. Combined with marginal (yet correct) offside calls, and goals being ruled out minutes after they were scored, opinion still remains divided on technology's introduction to football.

Liverpool midfielder James Milner summed up the thoughts of many in October 2019: 'Goal-line technology is incredible. Instant decision. Black and white. But it's very hard to use VAR when you've still got opinions on the decisions.' Milner's main complaint was that the 'atmosphere is being ruined', with sides scoring but celebrations, the 'explosion of noise', being halted by waiting for VAR's final call.[304] In November 2019 referees' chief Mike Riley acknowledged there is 'still a long way to go' before VAR can be considered

---

303 BBC, 'World Cup 2018: VAR system "fine-tuned" after criticism', *BBC Sport* (29 June 2018) https://www.bbc.co.uk/sport/football/44658757

304 *The Guardian*, 28 October 2019

a complete success. As he says, 'we will all be debating VAR until we become accustomed to it'.[305] VAR – here to stay and certainly a major moment in the history of the beautiful game!

---

305 *The Guardian*, 22 November 2019